PRACTICAL REFLECTIONS ON FIGURED SINGING

by

Giambattista Mancini

*The editions of 1774 and 1777 compared,
translated and edited by Edward Foreman*

MASTERWORKS ON SINGING, Volume VII

*PRO MUSICA PRESS
2113 W. Kirby
Champaign, Illinois*
MCMLXVII

TABLE OF CONTENTS

iii

INTRODUCTION

Practical Reflections on Figured Singing is one of the cornerstones of our understanding of the art of singing in the eighteenth century. With Tosi's *Observations,* it forms the sole technical reference to the teaching of the great master-teachers of that era.

Giambattista Mancini was born in Ascoli, in Piacenza, Italy, 1716, and died in Vienna, 4 January 1800. He was by turns a student of Leonardo Leo, Antonio Bernacchi, and Padre Martini. Very little is known of his life before 1760, when he was called to Vienna as royal singing master to the Imperial Court. His fame and excellence must have been known and appreciated widely to have been picked for a position which carried so much honor, and which was so widely sought. The book which he wrote and published in 1774, *Pensieri e Riflessioni Pratiche Sopra il Canto Figurato,* upholds the wisdom of that choice, even to the present day. Burney, who met Mancini in Vienna in 1772, was excited about the prospect of having a book on singing by such an excellent master. Among his students, Mancini numbered many renowned dilletantes, and the Princess of Parma and the Archduchess Elisabeth were especially noted for their trills, portamentos and suavely executed passages of agility.

The *Practical Reflections* appeared in Paris in 1776, under the title *L'Art du Chant Figure,* translated, as Mancini himself tells us, by M. Defaugiers. In 1777 a new edition was brought forth in Milan [See Appendix I], and called the Third Edition, which probably takes into account the French translation as the Second Edition. In fact, only the editions of 1774 and 1777 were prepared under Mancini's guidance. In 1796 a new French edition, *Reflexions Pratiques sur le Chant Figure* came forth; and in 1807 a further Italian edition was brought out, *Metodo Per Ben Insegnare D'Apprendere L'Arte del Cantare, Ossiano Osservazioni Pratiche su Questa Nobile e Difficile Arte,* including a letter from Mancini to a "Conte N.N." Johann Hiller in his *Anweisung Zum Musikalisch Zierlichen Gesang,* 1780, incorporated some sections of Mancini's text, and it has since been translated into German in its entirety. The first English translation seems to have been that of Pietro Buzzi, published in 1912. This edition suffered from a translator unfamiliar with Italian type faces of the seventeenth century, in addition to many undiscussed scholarly problems regarding interpretation, biography, and so forth. It seemed that the time had come for a more reliable, more useful translation, and I hope that I have provided it.

The edition of 1912 utilized only the text of the edition

of 1777; I have used both texts, feeling that there was something uniquely personal about Mancini's treatment of the subject in the first edition, and something more universally applicable in the later edition; I hope thereby to have made it more useful for both the practical musician and the researcher

Questionable words of a technical nature are discussed in Appendix II; Biographical Data on the persons mentioned by Mancini are included in Appendix III, where that information could be obtained. To my knowledge this information has not heretofore been available in any single reference work.

The assistance of numerous persons and institutions has been invaluable. I wish to express special appreciation to the Civico Museo, Bologna, from whose original copies of the editions of 1774 and 1777 my microfilms were made, with the kind permission of the Signor Direttore; to the Staff of the Library of the University of Illinois for their assistance in biographical research; to my patient typist; and most of all, to my wife and family, who have not always been sure I was at home unless the typewriter was being pounded.

Champaign, Illinois   *Edward Foreman*
May 1967

PRACTICAL REFLECTIONS ON FIGURED SINGING

by

Giambattista Mancini

Vienna, 1774

TO HER ROYAL HIGHNESS, MME. MARIA ELISABETTA, ARCHDUCHESS
OF AUSTRIA, ROYAL PRINCESS OF HUNGARY, AND OF BOHEMIA, ETC.

THE AUTHOR:

[A] *Born under the auspices of Your Royal Highness, and
coming in part from the natural talent and delight in your
employ, nothing is lacking in this slim but fortunate little
work of mine on the Art of Singing, except precisely that
honor which you have today granted, of publishing it with
your august name in the front. The simple rules described
here, without exaggerations of style, and the verbal instructions emanating from long experience in my profession, come
together quite successfully to form the taste of Your Royal
Highness, opportunely perfecting those luminous talents and
those happy graces of the voice with which nature so devoted-
ly endowed you. Strengthened by following certain exercises,
and by reflection upon the precepts of art, Your Royal Highness arrived at execution of the most complicated refinements
with that precision and bravura which only rare examples may
adduce from such triumphant ability. Taking as illustrious
testimony that high satisfaction which was aroused in the
Imperial Court during the periodical experiments when your
vocal progress was tested; we recall once more the universal
applause of all those judicious and intelligent persons who
gathered for the honor of hearing you. Deign, August Princess, to accept with pleasure the public tribute of frank
praise which I dare to present Your Royal Highness, as much
for just complacency as for the result of my own devotion.
My every care will invariably be directed toward meriting
the precious continuation of your high favor, and to dis-
charging in the best way the duties of the position with
which I have been honored by your most illustrious court.*

1

This small treatise on figured singing is nothing more,
Oh Readers, than a happy collection of my thoughts and of my
practical reflections in the course of many years in the
music profession: this collection was begun for my private
study, was pursued by the encouragement of friends and students; and now I do not know what good destiny brings it to
light. If you wish my candid sentiment on it (such as it
is), I would say that, in so much as it is directed at the
instruction of the young and to the improvement of the nobility of the Art, that youth will find food for thought here,
and the professionals, delight. [A]

Music, according to common opinion, takes its name from
the word "muse," and is defined as "the art of combining
sounds in a manner pleasing to the ear;" such is the art
which has always been taken as the most amiable and enjoy-
able of the liberal arts; on the contrary, I maintain that
if you wish to explore the principles of the combination of
sounds, and the reason for the feelings which are aroused
and moved in us, you must rather call it a "science."

The excellence and enjoyment of an art reasonably may
be deduced to arise from three springs, that is, from the
antiquity of its birth, the quality of the persons who take
it up and exercise it, and from the best effects which it
has produced.

The origin of music is very old [B]; I am not desirous
of recalling the famous inventor who would make my discussion
vain, and about whom many and many a devoted pen has written,
above all the immortal pen of Padre Master Giambattista
Martini, still living in Bologna, a brilliant man, a standard and light for the Musical Profession; through his history
and his publications he may be called the honor of our century and of his Order.

Perhaps in the first time of the world, Jubal was the
inventor, as we read in the Scriptures, or perhaps after the
Flood retreated, the Egyptians, as Diodorus says; or perhaps
the Arcadians, as Polybius says, were the inventors; or
Amphion, as Pliny says; or Dionysus, as the Greeks have it;
or others; for me it is enough to know that it remains truly
one of the most ancient of the arts, even if one does not
agree with Lucretius that it was born with the first men, who
learned how to sweetly modulate their voices from the beautiful natural concerts of the Angels.

Truly, who is there in the world who ignores singing,
whether they sing well or poorly? Singing is found everywhere that people speak. The soldier sings in War; the

shepherd sings in Peace; the very savages, who live among
their rocky wastes like beasts, have their songs, as Rousseau
reports in the last table of his musical dictionary. [C]

Praise of this art is not limited to the enjoyments of
antiquity; it enjoys everywhere the best reputation, that of
being common to and accepted by, every nation which sees the
sun, and loved by every rank of persons who live on the
earth. [D]

What can I tell you; how many, oh how many great men,
most holy; those of weighty cares, either political or military, those of the most rigidly thorny philosophies, attracted by the sweetness and goodness of singing, have stolen a
little time to learn the art and make it their own, not as a
profession, but as a talent and delight; adorning themselves
with toga, or sword, or knowledge no less than with the lyre,
and honoring art at the same time. David sang psalms while
playing the harp, Jeremiah sang his Lamentations to the
cither, and Cecilia her soliloquies to the organ. And Alexander the Great, and Titus and Hadrian and Marcus Aurelius,
all Emperors, were they not versed in this art, and powerful
protectors of this art?

The most holy Archbishop and Protector of Milan, St.
Ambrose, so applied himself to this art as to become the inventor of the cantus firmus, which takes from him the name
Ambrosian Chant, or Gregorian. [E] And the venerable abbot
Guido d'Arezzo brought understanding to figured singing, of
which we are speaking, through a new and clear system which
he left us.

I do not wish to bore the young, but I can no more neglect the honors of the art which I profess, than I can leave
out the persons who have honored it.

The Greeks and Romans have left testimony enough; Homer
assures us that Chirone taught music to Achilles. Cimone and
Epimanonde esteemed it equally glorious to be able to direct
a musical chorus well as to be able to guide a military exercise. Marcus Caecilius, Lucinius Crassus, Temistocles and
Appius Claudius, when returning from their victories, did not
value a triumph which was not accompanied by music.

[F] What more? Even rigid Philosophy became human
through the medium of this art. Pithagoras, according to
Laertius, set the study of music before many others, and cultivated it with the same attention as Geometry and Arithmetic;
and truly to such good effect that he was enabled, according
to Suedius and Boethius, to derive first the proportions of
the principal consonant intervals of music from the accidental sounding of three different blacksmith's hammers. Solon,
great master of philosophy, wished in his old age to learn
music. Socrates himself, believing one could not be a

3

perfect philosopher if he lacked musical knowledge, began at the age of seventy to have the rules taught him. [G]

The praise of the art is piled up in treatises by Plato, Aristotle, Cicero, St. Augustine; one calls it the Divine Discipline; another Celestial; one the pleasure, the joy, the relief of the condition of human misery; values and excellences all, which one cannot find associated with any other art. [H]

The best argument to prove the excellence and the value of this art is without doubt experience itself, which proves to every man through the wondrous effects which are produced in the human heart: by an occult divine force the heart is seized and turned and turned again by its talent. Now it disturbs, now speeds up, now fills with love, or pride, now moves to a smile and now to a tear, and all this is the result of the virtue of song.

The furious transposts of Saul, calmed by the harp of David: are they not a brilliant proof? And the madness of Alexander, aroused by Phrygian song, was calmed by Timotheus and the Lydian mode; today the horrible and black effects of melancholy, are they not dispersed with sound, with song? [I] A rare anecdote of the most cruel Hammurabi IV(1) should close this article.

This man, having taken Baghdad, ordered, without distinction as to age or sex, the death of all the inhabitants. Among these unfortunates there was a certain Schacculi, an accomplished Persian musician who begged so cleverly that he was able to have himself dragged before the throne of Hammurabi, to whom he spoke as follows: "I am not sorry to lose my life, but it distresses me that with me should perish so excellent an art as Music, which, if I lived, I flatter myself I might bring back to its perfection. Let me but have enough time to enable me to perfect this divine art, and should I succeed in arriving at the mark to which I aspire, I will die as happily as though I possessed your Empire."

He was ordered then to give a demonstration of his skill: for this he took in hand a Scheschadar (an instrument like a psaltery or harp) and accompanying its sound with his voice, Schacculi sang with great sweetness of the taking of Baghdad and the triumph of Hammurabi, so much so that the prince was reduced to tears, and not only stopped the slaughter of the people, but gave them back their liberty.

There is nothing in this work, unless studious youths and lovers of this beautiful art apply themselves with

---

(1) *Extrait de l'Histoire de l'Empire Ottoman par le Prince de Cantemir, imprime en Paris en 1743. Vol. 4 in 12mo al Tom. 3. nel Regno d'Amuratti alla nota K.*

judgement and industry, so that they may one day honor themselves, their native lands, and their art. Keep firmly in mind and in the heart, therefore, my candid advice, which is that one can never arrive at being a polished Virtuoso without good guidance; one will never be among the Great and universally esteemed, if to the harmonious quality of his singing he does not join the harmonious quality of good conduct; we know for a certainty that vices are abominable in every kind of person, but much more in those of us who are exposed to the public.

ARTICLE II: *OF THE DIFFERENT SCHOOLS, AND THE WORTHY MEN AND WOMEN, WHO HAVE FLOURISHED IN THE ART OF SINGING AT THE END OF THE CENTURY JUST PAST, AND STILL FLOURISH TODAY.*

[A] The conditions and systems which have directed the schools of this beautiful art are varied, as are the conditions and systems in any single school varied by the gifted master who wisely understands the quality and ability and genius of each scholar; that is not to say that every school and system can boast of virtuosi before the public; I believe all the progress of a great singer depends upon wise leadership and the careful direction of a worthy master who understands the talents of the youth he is teaching.

I must mention at this point that I have no intention of speaking of anything but the Italian national art of Figured Singing, which alone, in the judgement of every nation, is most apt to move the human heart. [B]

The most celebrated and famous of the renowned schools which have established a name for themselves in this area during the last fifty years are those of [C] Francesco Antonio Pistocchi in Bologna, Brivio in Milan, Francesco Peli in Modena, Francesco Redi in Florence, Amadori in Rome, and those of Niccolo Porpora, Leonardo Leo and Francesco Feo in Naples. [D] One cannot praise too highly the merits of these schools and of the students and professors. [E]

But to proceed in some kind of order, let us look over the valorous men who appeared with glory at the end of the last century. Cavaliere Baldassare Ferri was living then, born in Perugia; he had the most beautiful, most extensive, flexible, sweetest and harmonious of all the voices. He was a unique singer, prodigious and free from rivalry, heaped with honors and gifts by the Sovereigns of Europe, and after his death, by the Muses of Italy. "Nothing," his contemporaries wrote, "could express the beauty of his voice and the graces of his singing. He had in the highest degree all the characteristics of perfection in every style; he was gay, proud, serious, tender at will; his pathos captivated the heart. In one breath he sang a scale up and down two full octaves, trilling continuously, and marking all the chromatic steps with so much accuracy, even without accompaniment, that if the orchestra during the improvisation sounded the note which he was singing, whether flat or sharp, one would instantly hear an agreement of pitch so perfect as to surprise everyone." [F]

The celebrated singers Siface and Cavaliere Matteucci were singularly admired for their rare voices and for the way in which they sang to the heart. Matteucci, after having served with full satisfaction in the Court of Spain, aggravated by age, returned to his native Naples, where he still lived in 1730, and was in the habit of showing his devotion by singing in church every Sunday morning. This esteemed man, even when he was past the age of eighty years, had a voice so florid and so clear, and sang in every way with such flexibility and agility, that every listener, not seeing him, believed him a youth in the flower of his years.

The admirable Gaetano Orsini had a similar gift for preserving in his old age a florid, mellow [pastoso] and flexible voice, and he died with the best reputation for his service in the Imperial Court in Vienna.

Francesco Antonio Pistocchi, [G] at the end of the past century, was called by God to the cloistered life of the Fathers of the Oratorio in the city of Forli, but came after some time to establish his residence in Bologna. Here he opened a school of singing, assisting each scholar with such charitable love, and teaching with such sound doctrine, that it is enough to consider the results of his work, and what they accomplished in order to deduce his knowledge.

The first among his four famous scholars was Antonio Bernacchi of Bologna, my master, one who was not gifted with a good voice, as he himself admitted; his friends made him promise, for his own good to place himself completely under the direction of the aforementioned Pistocchi, who not only welcomed him with great affection, but began immediately to determine the course of study which he ought to undertake assiduously in order to obtain for himself those advantages which would prepare him for probable success. The obediant scholar did not hesitate to undertake any trial, no matter how disastrous, how painful, and to apply himself for a prescribed time, according to the precepts of the master, to whom he did not fail to go each day for wise counsel. During the time of this study he not only did not sing in church nor theater, but let no one hear him sing except his most intimate friends. He remained strong in his resolve as long as he received counsel from this same master, and until the time that he arrived at such perfection that he should be able to procure universal admiration. And such was the good effect which was produced by the assistance of such a great master, and the active and unwearied labor of a willing scholar. My pen would presume too much if it believed itself able here to relate all the praises which this great man earned. [H] It is enough for me to say that he was universally admired, and that he became one of the first figures in the Profession of Singing, as has been indubitably attested by all those who heard him - and they are many - who yet live. [I] The scholar should reap from this fact the

7

profitable reflection that an assiduous study under a great master can render a bad voice good. Antonio Bernacchi was not only one of the first figures in the Profession of Singing, but also emulated his own master, opening a school for the benefit of youth. [J] The great number of these are today dead, only Giovanni Tedeschi, called Amadori, the great Tommaso Guarducci, and the celebrated and well-known Antonio Raff being still alive.

These three professors, so universally distinguished from each other by the variety, taste and appropriateness of their styles, were able to unite themselves in such a worthy mode of living as to earn the grateful memory of the Profession.

Antonio Pasi of Bologna, likewise a scholar of Bernacchi, was celebrated for his skillful singing, and for a completely unusual taste, through the union of a solid portamento with the spinning out of the voice, and he introduced a solidity [*misto di granito*] composed of gracious gruppetti, mordents and tempi rubati, all done to perfection and in their appropriate places, the whole making an individual and arresting style. [K]

Giambattista Minelli, of the same city and school of singing, sang the range of contralto smoothly, with a noble portamento of the voice, to all of which was joined a profound knowledge which won him renown in his own vocal type. [L] [M]

Bartolino of Faenza was also a scholar of the aforesaid Pistocchi, and accompanied Antonio Bernacchi in his studies, becoming one of the leading figures in the Profession.

These four different scholars we see taught by one master, by varied methods and styles, as indicated by the natural inclination of each one of them. This example, known and understood, suffices to assure us that every great master is sure of guiding his scholars by whatever right way will lead them to become each one a perfect original. [N]

The value of being original is understood and will always be appreciated: such value will not be set upon the copy, no matter how perfect the resemblance. It is not for this reason that the imitator, who pleases for himself, is never criticized; rather, it is my opinion that he ought to receive admiration and applause; he ought also to thrust from himself all passion for picking out only one who is similar to himself, and ought with accurate justice be able to masquerade and imitate, otherwise he will never acquire the name of a perfect professor.

Senesino and Giovanni Carestini, born in Monte Filatrina in the Anconian Marches, distinguished themselves by their original singing and estimable acting; this latter was

8

brought at the age of twelve to Milan, where he took the
name Cusanino in gratitude for the help of the Cusani family.
Although his voice was beautiful by nature, he did not fail
to purify it by study, and render it apt in every style of
singing to such a sublime degree, that already in his youth
his ability and fame were established. He had a most rich
mind and a delicate discernment of the way in which every
part of his mind might be enriched, so that he never bragged,
nor remained satisfied or content. It happened one day that
a friend found him in the act of studying, and applauded his
singing; the good Carestini said to him: "Friend," he said,
"if I do not manage to satisfy myself, I shall not be able
to satisfy others;" he then repeated the aria so many times
that he was able to find the things which would give the
most pleasure; and because of this his singing was exquisite, exact, and sublime. He did not lack for acting ability, rather he studied it assiduously, not being personally
content until he had mastered all its diverse styles so perfectly that he was worthy of fame for this alone.

Now I will take an opportunity to record the memorable
ladies who flourished at the same time as these aforementioned celebrated professors. [O]

Vittoria Tesi Tramontini is without question worthy of
holding the first place; she was born in Florence, where she
received her first instruction in the profession of singing
from the celebrated *Maestro di cappella* Francesco Redi. She
then moved to Bologna, and continued her daily study under
the direction of the renowned Campeggi, not omitting at the
same time to frequent the school of Bernacchi. Thus she did
not lack the study which assured the possession of the art
of singing, and a perfect and exquisite method, and yet, ani-
mated by her natural genius, she resolved to acquire with
more tenacity the art of acting. She was correct in this
resolution, for she was adorned with all the rare prerogatives which so infrequently appear together, but were united
in her. An estimable and very complex personality, accompanied by a noble and gracious portamento; a clear and exquisite pronunciation; a sounding of the words according to
their true sense; the adaptability to distinguish one character from another as much through a change of facial expression as with appropriate gestures; complete intonation,
which did not vacillate in even the most fervent action, were
excellences so singular in her, and so perfectly guided by
her art, that she remained the one perfect mistress. This
lady merited such great fame and honor that finally in 1769
she was decorated with the Order of Faith and Constancy by
the King of Denmark, and she is the same lady who was the
mainstay of the Italian theater [P] in her time. If she had

9

not added the study of acting to her natural disposition, as she did, I do not believe that it would have revived, because she was gifted with rare talent; but not to such a degree that no other actress could equal her.

Next to her is Faustina Bordoni, wife of the very celebrated master Giovanni Hasse, called *Il Sassone* (1); she was born in Venice, where she learned the art of singing under the direction of Micaelangelo Gasparini of Lucca. The professor was not only perfect in his art, but became a very celebrated contrapuntalist under the direction of the celebrated and most gifted Antonio Lotti. He wrote several Theatrical Operas of fine and rare taste like his other gifts, and also conducted church music well. This singer, well guided by her master, developed a rare method, consisting of a distinct and purified vocal agility, which she used with incomparable facility, earning applause from the very first years in which she presented herself before the public. Her style of agility was so pleasing because it sounded to the very end, and in a way so new, and above all so difficult, in sustaining a passage with notes in sextolets, or even in triplets, and performing with such exact proportion, without ever slowing down in ascending or descending, giving to each its proportionate coloration, as is exactly necessary for the setting forth of each passage. The perfect and happy execution of this agility is extraordinary, and gives the character of a great professor to anyone who possesses it to perfection. Our Faustina Hasse sang with this rare method, so she could not be imitated. Besides this natural excellence of agility she had another kind of agility, accompanying with everything a fast and very solid trill and mordent. She had a perfect intonation, a secure knowledge of spinning forth the tone and sustaining the voice. The refined art of conserving and refreshing the breath, and the excellence of a finished taste. All of these were sublime gifts in her, perfectly mastered, and maintained through assiduous study, by which she attained a facile execution of great perfection, united to the just precepts of the art. If from all this emerges a complex perfection, one must also say that our *virtuosa* reaped approbation as her just reward, with universal esteem; so much is true, that she always received merited applause, and distinction in every place where she was heard. [R]

Francesca Cuzzoni, born in Parma, was a disciple of the distinguished Professor Francesco Lanzi, under whose direction

---

(1) *Giovanni Hasse, fortunately for our Profession still living, is so celebrated as a composer of Music, that one may justly give him the title of Supreme Writer.* [Q]

she became a most highly regarded singer, because she was gifted with a voice angelic in its clarity and sweetness, and because of the excellence of her style. She sang with a smooth legato; she acquired such a perfect portamento of the voice, united to an equality of the registers, that she not only carried away those who heard her, but also captured their esteem and veneration in the same moment.

This excellent lady lacked nothing which seems important to us, for she possessed sufficient agility; the art of leading the voice, of sustaining it, clarifying it, and drawing it back, all with such attention to perfection that she was given the valued name of "Mistress." If she sang a cantabile aria, she did not fail in fitting places to vitalize the singing with rubato, mixing proportionately with mordents, gruppetti, volatinas and perfect trills; [S] all of this together produced admiration and delight. Her voice was so given to exact execution that she never found any obstacle which she did not easily overcome; she used the highest notes with unequalled precision. She was the mistress of perfect intonation; she had the gift of a creative mind, and accurate discernment in making choices; by reason of these her singing was sublime and rare. This sublime quality and rarity of singing made her famous throughout Europe, and so all the best theaters vied with other for who should have her. She sang repeatedly in the principal cities of Italy, and the very respectable English nation, well knowing the worth of such a singer, had her come to London at least four times. The first time she went she was married to Pietro Sandoni, of Bologna, a celebrated *Maestro di cappella,* and a great professor of harpsichord and organ. This worthy man established himself in London with real credit, equal to that of the famous Frederic Handel; for this reason, the London public many times wished to hear them play together on two separate organs, with the usual friendly rivalry of two worthy professors. [T]

Gaetano Majorano, called Caffarelli, [U] was born in the province of Bari. In his youth he moved to Naples, where he applied himself so assiduously and with such rapidity to his studies, that he became admired very early by all of this most respected Profession. In the progress of time he went to all the various theaters of Italy, [V] from which came such reports of his good name and credit that he was distinguished as a worthy man. I shall not extend myself in enumerating his merits, since he is still alive and they are known throughout Europe.

Carlo Scalzi, from Genoa, found in the Profession such a worthy subject for study that he was esteemed among the number of first singers. Successively one can name such

11

celebrated singers as Giovacchino Conti, called Gizziello,
Agostino Fontana, Regginella, Domenico Annibale, Angelo Maria
Monticelli, Giuseppe Appiani, called Appianino, and Felice
Salimbene, all from Milan, and finally the two great tenors,
Gregorio Babbi of Cesena, and Angelo Amorevole of Venice. [W]

Among female singers who have proved excellent, [X] and
honored our Profession, one may justly list a certain
Peruzzi [Y]; Teresa Reutter, *virtuosa da camera* in the Imperial Court at Vienna; [Z] Caterina Visconti, called la Viscontina [AA]; Giovanna Astrua [BB], and la Mingotti. [CC] I
shall not dally in dealing at length with the virtues of each,
in order not to make this Article overlong, and because I am
certain that the reader already knows of their excellence
from other sources. I shall only say that these, beside
being gifted with beautiful voices, knew well exactly what
style of singing their natures inclined them toward, and
applying themselves to this certainty, and well-directed by
their masters, became each one a perfect original. [DD]

It is true that there are some today whom we count as
sustaining the honor and prestige of the art; for instance,
Rosa Tartaglini, wife of the great tenor Tibaldi, who by her
own choice abandoned the theater after a few years; and
Caterina Gabrielli, Lucrezia Agujari, Anna de Amicis, Elisa-
betta Teyber, Antonia Girella Aguillar, Antonia Bernasconi,
Caterina Leidnerin, known under the name Schindlerin, and
her neice, Marianna Schindlerin; Santarelli, Giovanni
Manzuoli, Filippo Elisi, Ferdinando Mazzanti, Giuseppe Aprile,
Gaetano Guadagni, Pasquale Potenza, Carlo Niccolini, Ferdinando Tenducci, Carlo Concialini, Giuseppe Millico, Antonio
Goti, Venanzio Rauzzini, Antonio Grassi, Giovanni Toschi,
Giuseppe Cicognani, Consort (1), Pacchierotti, and many
others. Since they are still living and acquiring great fame
and reputation for themselves, it would be presumptuous of
me if I believed I could enhance their reputations with my
panegyrics.

And here I am constrained to confess my amazement that
such worthy virtuosi can nevertheless have become established,
these who have sustained and do now sustain the honor of the
art, for in Italy music is decadent, there are no more
schools, nor great singers. There are still a few esteemed
masters, and still some few valorous scholars. I do not
know to what else may be attributed the real cause, since the
ancient systems have fallen into disuse, and the good customs
of the ancient schools no longer regulate our Profession. I
am certain that no school merits the name of a true school
except the Venetian Conservatories, the Neapolitan

---

(1) *Is this perhaps Gian Luca Conforti?* [*Ed. note*]

Conservatories, and the school of Cavaliere Bartolomeo Nucci at Pescia. [EE] This Cavaliere, through his devotion, has been the only one, for forty years and more, to continue the good system of the ancient masters. He does not instruct youth in expectation of money, but purely incited by glory and humanity. For this reason he does not admit to his school those whom he knows unable to finish, and those he does admit he teaches with such love and patience, that they necessarily become worthy and valuable. Thus from his school, because it is directed by a most honest and impartial master who lets neither fatigue nor lack of time interfere with the methodical instruction of his scholars, have come, and continue to come, the best students. Among these is distinguished, with much honor and glory to his master, the celebrated Mazzanti, who had the advantage of being for some time his scholar.

A like reason is not so easy to hope for from the other schools of our day, which (if I may say it) are almost become unions for the traffic, and mere shops. The directors of these have already introduced the evil custom of renting children for a time from their parents. And curing whatever is needed to bring the best from the scholar, and so that the allotted time will not pass unfruitfully, they cause them to fly over the rules of music, and teach them just enough to enable them to sing a few arias, and a motet or so, then they put them before the public to recover great wealth.

In this manner they remove the means of continued study, and soon their defects harden and become incorrigible; soon they are put into the provincial circuits, without regard to their tender ages, to seasons, to company, and this prejudices the health, the voice, the chest and the way of life.

How then could excellent professors emerge from such scholars? The reader can judge how desirable it would be if this type of school were removed entirely, and how beneficial to the youths it would be, if none were admitted as masters except those who know, and wish to put into practice, the true method of instructing, without personal gain, and with paternal affection.

In all the liberal arts the resulting scholars depend very much upon the knowledge of the master, and his good will to teach; but in singing schools, everything depends on it. If a painter, or sculptor, or an architect, or _maestro di cappella_ is not among the best, and cannot candidly communicate the correct understanding to all his scholars, in spite of that they can perfect themselves in everything the master has left unfinished and lacking. Such perfect examples of painting, sculpture, architecture and counterpoint can be found in this way, left by the best professors, that a good

13

talent finds it enough to take them for models, and may become a very good imitator by force of diligence. [FF]

It is not so in the art of singing. There do not exist, nor can there exist in this, the kind of monuments mentioned above, for the simple reason that a great singer cannot leave posterity a memorial of that inspiration, that method, that grace, and of that skill with which he alone embellishes his singing. One finds, it is true, vocal music written by the greatest masters, and long ago perfectly executed by some celebrated singers: but in such a monument one finds only the concept of a simple cantilena, or a simple passage indicated, enough to let the great singer have full liberty in embellishing the composition in accord with his talent, and thus, if the scholar wishes to take this as a model, he sees it only as a skeleton, and it neither reveals by what means, with what fire, nor with what skill it was set forth, and ought again to be executed.

Let us take in hand, for example, an aria sung by the celebrated Farinelli, and separately written out, those variations with which he used to embellish it. We will certainly discover from this his talent, his knowledge, but we cannot ascertain what was his precise method, which made his execution so perfect and so amazing, for this cannot be expressed in notation.

Then if this method, this fire, this skill, which renders the vocal music so ambiguous, cannot be explained by notation, but only with the voice, and through the teaching of a master, is the necessity not evident for having vocal schools be always directed by the most worthy and talented professors, since only from these can come others who in turn will be able to communicate to studious youths the refinements of the Art?

It is certain that every great professor can form excellent students every time he takes pains to inquire first to what method of singing his scholar has a natural inclination, and then wishes to lead him patiently through it, and regulate him, establishing by good principles that style which he knows is best suited to his talents.

However, one cannot promise the scholar that good method, and the single-minded patience of the master in rendering it excellent, will be enough. He ought above all else to adopt an unflagging diligence for learning, persuading himself that every doctrine and direction of his instructor is the best; he should never disdain salutary advice, nor capriciously reject it, deploring his stolidity, because the damage which that can do is irreparable. Too many believe themselves able without maturing enough, and without proportionate study, to sing a few arias written for Gaetano

14

Majorano, called Caffarelli, for Giovacchino Conti, called
Gizziello, for Ferdinando Mazzanti, professors all well-known
for their rare merit, acquired through assiduous study directed by profound knowledge, judgment, art, and the experience
of many years: these undertakings are poisonous to youths,
and produce the worst effect, which, taking the scholar
abruptly from his ordinary and regular method, ensnare him
in such errors, that what began as mediocre becomes bad.
Every scholar should subject himself to the highest discipline, and ought to put away his caprices and pretensions.
If he will accept these healthy counsels, he can hope for a
full success, through which he may place himself in the position of becoming distinguished, esteemed and beloved.

ARTICLE III: *OF THE STRICT OBLIGATION OF PARENTS, AND OF THE CHRISTIAN PRECAUTIONS WHICH THEY OUGHT TO TAKE BEFORE DESTINING A SON FOR THE ART OF SINGING.*

[A] The facility with which many parents, especially in our Italy, destine their sons indiscriminately to this art, has always moved my soul to the liveliest compassion; thus, now that the occasion presents itself, I should, under the title of Christian charity, remind all parents of the strict obligation they have to expose their sons to the judgment of worthy savants, and to have them undergo a rigorous examination to assure themselves that they have been furnished by nature with all the necessary qualities demanded by singing, before they begin instruction, that they not place them in danger of being forever unhappy.

If I were a moral theologian, or a politician, I should stop at this point to examine if it were not a good thing to remove completely this abuse every time I found it not beneficial to the young.

According to the material which I propose to discuss, it is enough to say that one cannot begin when the child is too young, since in this case one is uncertain what disposition he may have toward singing. And if this is not done, it may be that the youths will be rendered useless to themselves, and to their native land, because placed in a position where they cannot embrace another profession, at least with any probable good results.

Thus no child should be destined to vocal music unless he has benefited by nature's gift of a beautiful voice, united to good talent, which is absolutely necessary in order to hope for good results. Not everyone can distinguish these in every case, for which reason I mention the decision of the savant and the professor.

The father is not brilliant enough, because not learned in the art, to be able alone to make such a decision, even though he may have heard his son sing a canzonetta with some excellence; but he ought to seek the counsel of a professor, who has the capacity to decide, and the probity not to cheat. Such a one will be able to say if the child is exempt from those defects of nature which would form obstacles to good results in singing.

This decision is not easy to make, [B] and it is easy enough to cheat in making it. It is necessary to have particular understanding about the voice, and how it is formed and how it is modulated. The common people believe that he who has an elevated chest, and can yell loudly, has the qualities necessary to come out a good singer. The strength of

16

the voice depends, it is true, upon the quantity of air which is expressed from the lungs, depending on how ample these are; and if the trachea is broad, and the larynx, so the tone of the voice is great, which is born from the pressing out of the air from the cavity of the thorax. It is also true, as the physiologists say, that the two lungs are instruments that contribute to speaking and singing with greater or lesser force as required, in as much as they and the chest are more or less ample and capacious for receiving and expelling the air introduced into them; but at the same time, one must say that it is just as certain that the lungs are not the true organs which form speech and voice. These are formed in the throat and in the mouth by the flowing back and forth of the air in passing through these parts at the time of inspiration and expiration. The air from the lungs works over the larynx in singing in the same manner as it works over the head of the flute, which one leans against the lips to play. It is not the lungs which sing; these do nothing except provide the material, that is, air; in the same way it is not the air that renders the tone of the flute pleasing, but the fingers which give it the diverse modulations. Thus the organs of the voice are the larynx, the glottis, the uvula, the palatal veil, the tongue, the teeth and the lips, and these are the parts which give the diverse inflections to the voice in singing.

The better these parts are organized, the more beautiful, strong and clear will be the voice. It will open in singing through varied pitches, high and low; it will stop, and it will shimmer through the many inflections, that is, in the various manners in which the air is expressed through the larynx. In speaking these organs are quiet and natural, but in the action of singing they are held to constant toil, and the most fatigue is in the muscles of the larynx: these direct the voice, condensing to produce the high notes and dilating for the low notes. A proof of what I say is to be clearly found in birds. These birds that have the narrowest and most compact epiglottises are those that sing well: those that have large ones in proportion to their bodies do not sing at all, or simply shreik.

And so I conclude that the elevated chest alone, and the power to shout at high pitches are not qualities sufficient for good results in singing. It is necessary that the organs of the voice be perfect, for if these are imperfect by nature, or through some illness which is not correctable, the singing will always be bad; that child who is directed by a good master has much more hope of good results to the extent that the organs named are well-formed.

For this reason the master should examine to see if the

17

epiglottis is free and not pressed down by the enlarged thyroid gland, commonly called goiter; and that the action of the small muscles of the larynx is not impeded by the *glandule summamassillari* or by the enlargement of the *amigdales*. He should observe the uvula and the soft palate attentively; and whether there is any tumor on the palate, or an unusual opening; if the tongue is loose and agile; whether the lips close equally; or whether the chin sticks out so far as to deform the good symmetry of the mouth; or scarcity mars the even-spacing of the teeth. He should note the good form of the nose, whether it is flattened or protrudes too much.

When the professor has made all these observations of the youth and found him perfect in all the parts, then can the father destine him to music with hope of good success; but if he is defective in one part alone, he ought not to hope for a good result; for every one of these defects will ruin the voice, and is incurable. It is very true that the glands of the neck [tonsils] may be removed; but it is also true withal that the voice will remain always defective [C]. I have observed this in Naples in three persons [D]. The celebrated surgeon Francesco Picillo removed their throat glands masterfully with two knives of reed, but this did not improve their voices.

So then if fathers wish to destine some one of their sons to the art of singing, let them destine only those who have good and beautiful voices, I mean to say those that have a sonorous body, are vigorous, flexible, agile, full [*pastoso*] and of rich range.

[E] I do not deny that a voice gifted with a vigorous register is estimable, and I admire it myself, but only when the extension accords with nature; never when either the master or the scholar presumes to make it by brute strength; Eh! let nature never be let to subject herself to Man, when Man wishes to conduct her beyond the limits she has prescribed herself; thus it is with the voice of the scholar, which should be lead by the wise master in that way, and by that method, adapted to the disposition of the voice, and to the capacity with which it is furnished, without pretending miracles.

Having made all these observations regarding the voice, the fathers should observe as well whether their sons have other defects of the body, although not related to the voice; how much these need interfere is a decision for surgeons and the experts in the art who are making the examination. One last thing I should say is that a youth with a handsome person, with good features and a pleasant aspect, even with mediocre talent, is well received by the Public; but on the contrary, if he is not excellent in singing, and surprises, a

youth with a marred body and face will be mocked everywhere,
and operating prudently, he should not be destined to singing.

ARTICLE IV: *OF THE VOICE OF THE CHEST AND HEAD, OR FALSETTO.*
[A]

[A] This article, although brief, nevertheless contains
a remarkable doctrine for the young; and I ask them to reflect diligently upon it.

The voice in its natural state is ordinarily divided
into two registers, one of which is called the chest, the
other the head or falsetto. I say ordinarily, because there
are rare examples in which one has received from nature the
most unusual gift of being able to execute everything in the
chest voice. I am speaking only of the voice in general divided into two registers, as commonly happens.

Every scholar, whether he be soprano, contralto, tenor
or bass, can ascertain for himself the difference between
these two separate registers. It is enough, if he begins to
sing the scale, for example if he is a soprano, from sol on
the third line [soprano clef] and going to c-sol-fa-ut [B]
on the fourth space, he will observe that these four notes
will be sonorous, because they belong to the chest; should
he wish to pass to D-la-sol-re, if the organ is not strong,
and is defective, he will give it only with pain and fatigue.
[C]

[D] Now this mutation is nothing but the changing of
the voice,which has arrived at the end of the first register,
and entering the second finds it by necessity more feeble.

[E] This chest voice is not equally forceful and strong
in everyone; but to the extent that one has a more robust or
more feeble organ of the chest, he will have a more or less
robust voice. In many the natural voice, or chest voice,
does not extend beyond B-mi; and many others will be able to
ascend as far as E-la-mi. [F]

[G] So art must remedy the defects of nature, for with
assiduous study youths may equalize the disparity in registers: hence that singer is mistaken when, speaking of his
voice, he says that it betrayed him in this or that situation, and calls it a "rope" or an "unfriendly voice." He
should rather say that he has himself betrayed his own voice,
because he gave no thought in the first years of study to
the union of his chest voice to that of the head.

[G] Have no doubt that of all the difficulties that one
encounters in the art of singing, the greatest by far is the
union of the two registers: but to overcome this is not impossible to him who will seriously study how it is to be done.

[G] Art and study are the only means for correcting certain defects of nature, in which, therefore, nature is flexible. This part, and this union of the two registers is so
important for consideration, and of such difficulty in the

Profession, that I have decided to reason it out extensively with you in another article, and give you those rules practiced by the best masters, by following which I have found how to produce this desirable union of the two registers.

I will end this article with a charming paradox, which will amaze you; I say that there may be natural defects which are more beautiful and more attractive in the voice when they are not corrected by art. Give me a veiled [*velata*] voice, which has enough body to be heard in any place no matter how large; it entices, pleases and softly seizes the human heart by means of its marvelous thick color; never crude, never strident.

However, I say let this virtuous natural defect, dimness [*appannata*] be heard only in the soprano or contralto and never in a tenor or bass; because these last two natural voices, as the sustenance and foundations of the harmony, ought to be sonorous, robust, and virile; and the veiled voice cannot ever be so, so behold how nature brings good out of ill, and we bring good out of defects through study, and let us then emulate nature in art.

ARTICLE V: *ON INTONATION*

[A] Every writer ought, according to the best rules, to guard against contradicting himself: if I said in Article III that only those youths with good voices should study the art of singing, I did not mean by that that everyone should indiscriminately apply himself just because he possessed a good voice, or that this sole gift is enough for good results, if other defects are present, and yet he has a good voice. For there are still defects which render singing unpleasant, no matter how good the voice; why? because some basic fundamentals are lacking.

There is nothing more insufferable and more inexcusable in a singer than bad intonation, and one will tolerate throaty or nasal singing more often than bad intonation. Since perfect intonation is the basic fundamental of harmony, and this is composed of the perfect agreement of consonances, if one of these consonances wanders from the utmost accuracy, the perfection of the whole harmony is immediately destroyed; the voice being by far the principal part of vocal music, if it be out of tune, the harmony of the accompanying instruments is ruined at the same moment, although they may be perfectly in harmony among themselves. All other defects may be in some way covered up by strength of art and study, at least far enough that they will not be noted except by one who has studied singing; but bad intonation cannot be masked, and even the inexpert will notice it, if they have the slightest alertness of ear. [B]

Bad intonation can arise from natural causes or accidental. That type can be traced to nature, when the studious youth has not been gifted with a perfect ear. Such a youth cannot have success in singing; for no one can succeed in changing a poorly formed organization of the body, in the manner that one can in an organ, where the pipes may be pushed in or drawn out, until the proper voicing is found. [C]

Bad intonation produced by accidental causes is correctable, and lasts no longer than the cause itself, which is usually a temporary indisposition of the body. It is the duty and burden of the professor to know which of these two causes produces the bad intonation in his scholar. This judgement is not difficult to make: but one must not hurry and make it without reflection; it is necessary, in order not to fool oneself, to have the youth sing pitches more than once on different days, and at different hours. If he is always out of tune, and does not himself realize he is singing a false pitch, but only when he is corrected and started again by the master, one can frankly judge that the defect is one of nature, arising from the imperfect organization of the ear. This being, as I have said, irremediable, it makes all study, and every effort useless, which one would wish to try to correct such a defect, and the honest professor can do nothing in such a case but inform the parents, so that they may destine the youth right away to some other science or art, without the useless loss of his good time in this school.

If, however, the youth who has sung out of tune today sings better tomorrow, and he himself shows signs of knowing his errors most of the time that he makes them, one cannot doubt that the bad intonation comes from an accidental cause; which, when it is removed, will no longer cause a bad effect. In this case the master should not despair of good results with his scholar, but ought often to point out attentively what the cause is, in order to make the best use of his opportunities and the surest remedies.

These accidental, or temporary causes of bad intonation are ordinarily either illness of the stomach, or an indigestion caused by intemperate eating, or other disorder. The wise master, having uncovered the true cause, ought seriously to correct it, and admonish the scholar who has voluntarily brought on a disorder: and he ought to treat the case with charity, if it be a weakness of the chest or stomach, and have him sing in the mornings and at critical hours in mezza voce, or he will encourage the ruination of everything.

To the two above-mentioned causes of accidental bad intonation, I now add another: distraction; this is most easy to correct, being a disattention and distraction of the thoughts of the scholar, who instead of listening to the harpsichord and attending to his pitches, becomes diverted, and lets his mind run to disassociated things; he recalls his mind at the point that the master starts him over, as though aroused from sleep, takes the tone again; and sings perfectly in tune.

The other usual cause of bad intonation originates when the scholar, singing to the accompaniment of a small spinet, or muted instrumentation whose sounds are overwhelmed by the voice in such a way that the scholar, not hearing perfectly the intonation of the instruments, falls into the bad practice of not being attentive to the perfect intonation, and, to speak frankly, always sings badly out of tune. [D]

I shall make a brief digression at this point in order not to deprive you of an anecdote of considerable value. A voice already formed is out of tune with itself; this may arise from two reasons: either it was not well chosen, or it was not well used. Reflect indeed, that a youth, whose voice is not well-chosen, and who does not have the art of

23

u sing it well, will hear his voice get bigger in the years of his greatest strength; and about the age of thirty five he will hear this same voice begin to get smaller, and sing naturally out of tune, a situation he cannot relieve, but rather he makes the defect worse by the use of another defect which manifests itself when he pushes the breath and strengthens by force the bellows of the voice; and note then that the intonation is very uncertain, the clarity and lightness of the voice are taken away, anxiety and anguish increase and the suffering of he who sings is equal to that of him who hears the singing.

Let us return to our path. When experience has once indicated the disposition and capacity of the scholar with respect to intonation, and found him able and disposed to success, he ought to pursue the following, to become strengthened at the same time, and solfege notes in every degree, observing with scrupulous attention that they are perfectly in tune: after this study should follow that of solfeging the notes that form regular leaps; and these first obstacles overcome, he ought to sing with equal attention in mezza voce according to the following rules. If the scholar sings soprano, he ought little by little to acquire the high notes, which are so necessary for adding a suitable extension of range to the voice. [E] Beside this, in proportion as the voice becomes formed, he ought to be certain that it takes on equal strength in the middle and lower notes, in order that an equally useable register be formed from them. The notes of the middle are by nature homogeneous and pleasant; l ikewise the deeper notes, because they come from the chest. The high voice is more difficult to master because it is strident in this condition. [F] So the scholar ought not to neglect to treat this portion of the voice with due sweetness to form a complete register.

The obstacles encountered in putting a voice onto the road to perfect intonation are not a few; and to overcome them requires great fatigue and attention of him who studies. [G] It would help not a little if every scholar read in the highly esteemed book by Pier Francesco Tosi, the explanation in Chapter Twelve which he gives on the major and minor seconds, in order to know precisely the quantity of the intervals, or of the commas of which they are composed. He gives as an example that if a soprano sings the high D-la-sol-re sharp like the E-la-fa, anyone with a good ear will hear that he is out of tune, because the latter is sharp; for this reason we must be careful not to err. [H] Whoever regulates his study with these very essential rules, will perfect his intonation securely; he who neglects this study, or abandons himself to his own caprice, will never succeed.

In older times they practiced in all the schools of Italy
a system of musical notation so extravagant and laborious
that it obliged the poor student to study many years in
order to make himself in any way its master; and this
method had to be scrupulously observed. This system not only resulted in an extraordinary fatigue in the scholar, but
caused him more errors in intonation because he gave so much
attention to the notational system. The celebrated and much
renowned Gaetano Greco of Naples, master in one of the conservatories of that city, was the first to simplify the
above-mentioned notation for his scholars, reducing it to a
much easier system; for he had often seen that a student,
while taking a lesson, believing he was doing well, gave
more attention to the notation than to the intonation. With
impatience he used to lift his hands from the harpsichord,
and turning to the scholar, say, "Sing the note in tune, call
it the Devil if you wish; but sing the note in tune." [I]
This shows clearly that this great man gave his attention
to the pure essentials and was not led astray. This same
system ought to be generally embraced in order to render it
easier, and of less fatigue to the scholar; for this reason
it is my opinion that the masters ought to observe when the
scholars read and name the notes easily, and then without
delay pass to vocalises; because to do otherwise will give
rise to the disadvantage that the continual naming of the
notes displaces the true position of the mouth; whereas the
second system establishes intonation, clarifies the voice,
facilitates agility and strengthens the vowels.

In the year 1761 the justly-famed Maestro Hasse, called
il Sassone, moved to Vienna in Austria, to write his opera,
Alcide in Brivio; and reasoning with me on the method of the
system of notation he praised to me a new rule which he recognized as being good, that he had seen practiced with
great profit by the Canon Doddi of Cortona. I asked him to
obtain an instructive example, and the kind Signor Maestro
lost no time in writing to his friend, who complied by sending a clear example with the following inscription: "Demonstration, showing how to give practical instruction in solfeging in all keys with one single notational system."

# *Pa.b*	# *Bo.b*		# *Tu.b*	# *De.b*	# *Na.b*		
ut C	*re* D	*mi* E	*fa* F	*sol* G	*la* A	*si* B	*ut* C

The first seven syllables [J] or monosyllables in-
scribed over the seven diatonic or natural keys of the harpsichord can be used to form the scale for solfeggio for the
voice of the soprano or contralto, beginning with low C-sol-
fa-ut and repeating octave by octave; if used for the voice
of tenor or bass, one starts in their respective scales of
C-sol-fa-ut, which are the octave below, both in ascending
and descending using the ranges of the voice which sing the
respective parts. With these one can form all the scales
made of natural intervals, found on the harpsichord in
sevens, both in forward and retrograde progressions, in the
same way that the French say ut, re, mi, fa, sol, la, si; and
repeat ut, re, etc.; the other five syllables or monosyllables placed on the middle keys of the harpsichord between
the seven natural intervals serve to form the second scale
for reading and singing the chromatic notes, or, we should
say, the accidentals, for the sharp and the flat, in the
following manner, ut, pa, re, bo, mi, fa, tu, sol, de, la,
no, si, and this repeats ascending and descending to whatever note is destined, whether the voice is soprano, contralto, tenor or bass. With these monosyllables alone, reduced
to the number of twelve, one may solfege any musical composition, whether for singing or playing, whether in sharps or
flats, in whatever key, however many strange accidentals may
be found; because this system follows the rules of harmony
and melody. The unique and principal reason for this is,
that invariably above the fixed key of the harpsichord,
whether in a natural or chromatic tone, and where still in
use, and enharmonic tone, the name of that monosyllable is
always the same, where it has been assigned to aid the memory and the imagination in singing with the precise pitch or
sound of the keyboard. From all of this one perceives that
the scholar ought before all else to learn to understand the
tuning of the harpsichord, and of the notes corresponding to
his voice, and the master should inform him that, for example,
the same key which serves to express the sound of the sharp
of C-sol-fa-ut, or simply of the letter C, serves just as
well for the flat of D-la-sol-re, or we should say, the letter D; and it is the same for the one as for the other, that
one should say for both the sharp and flat, "pa," and in the
same way for the other semitones. Once the natural scale has
been learned, he should pass to exercises on the interval of
the third, the fourth, etc., and then to others composed of
all the tones and semitones, according to the discernment
of his teacher and his talent for learning, which may allow
for changes in this order. To clarify this method and con-
firm the reason given for the invariability of the spelling,
one adds that if a flat be given to the notes E-la-fa and

-fa; and also if to the notes already sharped in a key, as to F-fa-ut a higher sharp, or so to speak a double-sharp, one should read these accidentals with the same monosyllable which has already been affixed to that key, which ought to express the flat or double-flat; or the double-sharp for example, if it is on F, one should pass from F sharp to make the double sharp on G-sol-re-ut natural, the name of which note should be sol, because that is the note fixed for that pitch, etc., and so for the flat on natural pitches, and the double flat on accidentals. According to my way of thinking, the rule is quite simple, and useable; because once the scholar has learned the spelling of the natural octave, it remains only to add the other five monosyllables, which serve for sharps and flats; this will surely give him an easy success because the same keys being on the harpsichord will facilitate his mastery.

The masters of Germany employ a similar system with syllables in their idiom.

All of this, if the masters be rigidly observant, will lead to each note being perfectly in tune.

I have myself experimented with this and found it both good and easy; and so I have faithfully described it for the profit of studious youths, without pretending to make the decision whether it was the best of all the rules in use; for this I place myself completely at the mercy of the wise. [K]

ARTICLE VI: *ON THE POSITION OF THE MOUTH, OR, ON THE MANNER OF OPENING THE MOUTH.*

Since I have set forth faithfully my own thoughts and the meditations made for the development of the voice apt to the profession of singing in all these articles of mine; so in this one I wish more than the others to reflect my faithfulness, with which I shall explain the rule for the position of the mouth; [A] rules which I have drawn from my masters drop by drop, and from my own simple experience of many years. [B]

Before entering on the point of the true and good position of the mouth, I will say that the defects and false positions which I have found among scholars, in all justice, are for the most part the fault of guilty masters. And it is the first precept for all of these, who put themselves to teach, and become masters of singing, that they should not instruct if they do not first recognize that they are furnished by nature with those gifts and that recognition and wisdom, which perfectly form a master. He should have a penetrating understanding for recognizing all the defects in a scholar, and a firm knowledge for knowing how to correct them and emend them, [C]: This capacity is such that it can only be gained after long study, study made under the direction of Professors of tested worth. [D]

[E] The natural gift most necessary to a master is that he be able to communicate well, that he may communicate to the scholar the rules of the art in the most simple and plain manner; a gift that nature does not give liberally, and a difficult and rare thing to acquire by study.

Certainly it is desirable that a scholar should have the good fortune to be instructed by a master who unites wisdom and natural gifts within himself; and he is indeed fortunate if he encounters a master who is facile, loving, patient, tireless, who understands his nature and the disposition of his talents. I do not speak of the other qualities necessary to a master, which are many and many, in order not to betray a youth given into his care, thinking that it is enough to have touched on those which are merely desirable in a master, and I shall now pass to three common defects.

The first defect is, to open the mouth wrongly, and seems at first to be the very easiest to correct, but this defect, no matter how common, is not the easiest to correct. The first thing which the master says to the scholar when he sings, and when he sings again, and in a low voice and in a high voice, is: "Open the mouth:" and he believes thus to have satisfied his duty; Not so in my judgement; it is

28

necessary to explain with grace to the poor inexpert and raw youth, what is precisely the true position of the mouth; and he should come back again to explain it, which is the whole point. *Principiis obsta.*

It is necessary that the student learn this good principle, and know how to open the mouth well; and know how to open it according to the rules, and not at his fancy. [F]   I value this knowledge of how to open the mouth well in a beginner, and the knowledge of how to place it well, so much because it is the source for the clarity of the voice and the neatness of the expression; thus on the contrary the defective position of the mouth spoils the voice absolutely, renders the cantilena disgusting, the singer ridiculous and repulsive because of the change which it makes in the face.

The false positions of the mouth are numerous enough; I shall note here only the most common, and finally give the rules which I believe to be the most certain to give the true position of the mouth.

One has seen many youths who, having heard "Open the mouth" repeated endlessly, open it, so that it seems they have opened a small furnace in the mouth, and in this action they look like nothing more nor less than Maskers from Fontana; but if such as these by bad luck encounter an unskilled dd master, who does not know how to correct them, they will never be able to perceive for themselves their immature judgment, which has reduced them to intemperate opening of the mouth, and thrown the voice back into the throat, and even less will they be able to perceive that the fauces being strained thereby, that natural clarity so necessary for the facile emission of the voice from the organ will in consequence be completely cut off. Hence there remains the poorly conceived placement of the mouth in the uncorrected scholar, and the poor man will sing, but with a voice that is suffocated, crude and heavy.

On the contrary, one observes others who believe that they open the mouth correctly, and they open it, but not enough. . .or give it a round form. . .and to compound the error. . .they put the tongue on an equal basis with the lips. This monstrous position produces three monstrous effects: first, instead of putting the voice into the air, they carry it into the throat: [G] second, it makes the youth sing viciously in the nose; and for the third, it makes the pronunciation lisping and stammering. The reason which experience gives is, that in the first case since the tongue is not lying in its accustomed place, the emission of the voice cannot be sonorous, because it strikes the palate and remains choked in the throat. In the second case the same reason pertains, because the emission of the voice is impeded by the

29

enlargement of the tongue, and instead of the defect of the
throat, acquires the vice of the nose. [H]   In the third case
finally, it is very natural that pronouncing with the enlarge
tongue, it is necessary that the inconvenient deformity
of stammering or lisping pronunciation should arise.

There are many who sing with their teeth closed and firm
ly so. To sing thus between the teeth is the greatest defect; it is a defect that completely betrays the voice, because one cannot hear its extension, and it does not retain
the neatness nor the clear articulation of the words.

Now such defects, once introduced into a youth, are in-
emendable: defects which defile the voice, since they seem
to be from the mouth of the directing master, and a rule of
singing; in the manner that the mouth is arranged, and in wha
guise it is formed, the voice resounds; but it ought to be
accompanied by natural strength in the chest and by the right
position of the throat, and will be read further on. Thus
it is that the corrections of those masters will always be
useless when they declaim saying: "You open the mouth too
much; and you too little; you still sing between your teeth."
[I] Let the master speak the rules precisely, and show vis-
a-vis what is the true and perfect position of the mouth.

I myself have always worked in the manner of a master
of dancing with my scholars, calling them one by one before
me, and after having arranged them in the proper position,
"Son," I say, "pay attention carefully. . .lift the head. . .
don't bend it forward. . .don't throw it back. . .but up-
right as is natural; thus the parts of the throat remain
supple; because if you hang the head forward, the parts of
the throat stretch suddenly, and they stretch if you lean it
back."

Keep in mind this rule of mine, which I make a gift to
you out of my good wishes. It is a rule which I received
from my Great Professors, and from the indefatigable study I
have made of all the reflections and admonitions which they
gave me; It is a rule proven by my experiments and those of
my scholars, adopted by all the good schools of antiquity and
by all the worthy modern professors. Here it is: Every
singer should position his mouth as he positions it when he
smiles naturally, that is, in such a way that the upper
teeth be perpendicularly and moderately separated from those
below; and now see how this same rule may be put into practical use.

Admittedly the master should make this rule known to his
student with evidence to show that this same position of the
mouth ought to serve for every articulation of the vowels;
to convince him of the absolute truth of this, have him pronounce the five vowels A,E,I,O,U, with the indicated position

of the mouth, and he will see that no change is necessary, except in pronouncing the O, and the U: [J] because in the pronunciation of the vowel O, an almost invisible change in the shape of the mouth is necessary: and in pronouncing the vowel U, one must move the lips forward together slightly; and in this manner the mouth does not go far from its natural position, but remains in its original form, and avoids and shuns all the pernicious affectations. One should not believe however, that for this reason the mouth should be deprived of its customary motion, and one should admit its necessity, not only to interpret the words, but also to expand and clarify the voice to that degree taught by the same art. [K]

To gain the most advantage from this, the scholar should accustom himself from the first to pronounce the notes, solfeging with the indicated position; and he should practice it even more when he passes to vocalising, distinguishing each vowel in its true and clear position. He must guard against contortions of the mouth, which resemble convulsions, and even more the motions of the whole body, as one sees too many Virtuosi through bad habits, in taking a high note, or making a gruppetto or even a passage, thinking, contorting, drawing back for help; and they do not realize that they are always developing stronger bad habits, and that their defects are becoming incurable; with this position of the mouth it becomes necessary for the throat to work in accord with it. To explain myself with greater clarity I shall say that the throat should let the voice loose with great ease, and ought to clarify each vowel not only in pronouncing it, but also in letting it slide out in the execution of every passage. That which is known as the defect of the throat, or the defect of the crude and smothered voice, always arises from the failure of the singer to derive and sustain the voice from the natural strength of the chest, but believes he will obtain the best effect solely by stretching the fauces. He is fooling himself, however, and should know for a certainty that this means alone is not sufficient to correct the voice, but is on the contrary absolutely pernicious, for the reason that if the fauces, as demonstrated in the third Article, are a part of the organ of the voice, this cannot come forth naturally and beautifully as long as the fauces are in a forced position, and impeded from working naturally. Every scholar must then tirelessly accustom his chest to give forth the voice with naturalness, and to use simply the light action of the fauces.

If the union of these two parts arrives at the required point of perfection, the voice cannot fail to be clear and melodious; but if they are disunited and do not work together

31

the voice cannot help but be unpleasant and full of defects, and consequently ruin the singing.

Be advised, that whatever the vowel may be, one must not betray it, placing it outside its appointed place, which may occur when it is pronounced or adapted, either too open or too closed.

If a false position of the mouth, as I have said, ruins the beauty of the voice and the expression, how much more will it contort and ruin the amiable visage of the singer; this situation should be taken very much into account, reflecting that his face is exposed to the eyes of the public which is hanging on his every vocal sound, and is in the act of praising him or censuring him. (Oh dear youths, learn with age, and when you calculate the various theaters in which one of our profession is exposed, and to how many vicissitudes and critical reflections, which seem small, but are great, you will admit what this can do.) How very great must be the industrious patience of your masters in correcting you when you fall into similar faults.

I do not doubt that every master, when his scholar makes a fault in opening his mouth, and makes a fault in the true pitch of a note, speaks to him thus: "Oh, that is not the true position, which I have taught you; that is a false pitch;" but I am sure that a correction so light and superficial is not enough to bring home the error to the youth, because he is able to understand why and how, and into which error he has fallen.

The easiest method, and one from which I have derived good results in making scholars aware of the proof of the errors they have committed, seems to me to be to imitate (counterfeit) faithfully the defect of the scholar. Thus the scholar can have proof of the error of singing through the nose, of singing in the throat, or with a thick, or crude, or heavy voice. Then, in hearing the master, when he overcomes the impact of hearing himself imitated, he remarks and confesses and condemns the errors in himself, which otherwise he would never have remarked, confessed nor condemned.

You should not believe that this method of imitation began with me, or with masters of our own day; it was this very method which Angelini Bontempo of Perugia mentions in connection with the celebrated Fedi. The worthy singers and teachers in Rome at the end of the last century often led their students to amuse themselves by going to the place where the famous echo resounded outside the Gate of St. Paul, and here they exercised with loud voices: the echo, which is nothing but an imitation of the same voice as is singing, exposed to the singer the defects from which he singing suffered; therefore the scholars could correct themselves and emend their errors with proof.

But it is not the defects of the voice alone which the scholar should emend, and the living imitation of the maestro helps in correcting at the same time all the other errors into which a scholar falls.

Defects of this second species are the bad position of the mouth. . .frowning of the forehead. . .rolling of the eyes. . .contortion of the neck. . .and of all the person. . . and similar things; in order to correct these I have adopted the habit with my scholars of constraining them to sing standing before me for all their lesson, and to sing from memory. From such a position I have been able to gain two advantages, one for myself, one for the scholar; I perceive and see more easily all his defects, and he exercises his memory; a necessary exercise, because singing from memory makes it easier to remove all the defects of a youth, since he is not obliged to stare intently with his eyes at the music. [L]

I close this article by recommending to the master no less than the scholar, the virtue of patience, which alone perfects the work. I have no doubt about the masters; about the scholars I have doubts, who easily believe these attentions to be small, because they neglect them, but small they are not; and how easily youth is irritated by the reprehensions of the master. Youths, do not let yourselves be irritated by the reprehensions which come from your masters, for they have their origins in love, and in the desire of seeing profit in you commensurate with the attention with which they teach you. Eh! do not become vain if you think you have genius, animation, discernment in perceiving, and in correcting yourselves immediately: these are deceptions, and phenomena to be pointed out *albo lapillo*.

ARTICLE VII: *ON THE MANNER OF DRAWING OUT, MODULATING AND STEADYING THE VOICE.*

It often happens that no matter how liberal nature has been in according to some youth a voice purged of every defect, of an extensive register, which one could call beautiful, she has been avaricious in not joining to it a sonorous body, robustness and flexibility.

A voice which lacks robustness is called a weak voice, and causes grave disturbance to the singer, who cannot make himself heard in a large place without pain and fatigue.

A sonorous body, or rather robustness of voice, is ordinarily a gift from nature, but can also be acquired by study and art.

The most useful means, and commonly held by masters to be the most valuable for obtaining robustness of voice where it is lacking, is to require such a scholar, at the time of his first study, to bring out all of his voice. (Sing full voice) Masters use this method without the least distinction of cases, on every sort of voice. But I reflect that since the qualities and constitutions of voices are varied, although they suffer from the same defects to the same degree, I believe that the indicated remedy, although in itself it may be good, cannot apply to every case and be a universal remedy. Rather for every case, and for every defect of the voice, there is a separate and particular remedy. [A]

The defective qualities of voices are many, of which I elect three which are the most vulgar and common, to suggest the corrections. One has by nature a voice strong, crude and strident; another a limited, weak and confused voice. Finally a third has one rich in extent, but very weak and slender in all its proportions. The two first are usually called *vocette.* (Little voices).

A voice that is robust, crude and strident has no other need than to become sweetened and purified. If one says to a youth who has such a voice. . ."Give all the voice;" surely he will not be able to correct the error; indeed, it will be made greater, because one cannot thus correct the bad quality, but rather increase the irregular and crude flexibility. In this case then, one ought to return to the scholar that quality of voice which is proportionate to his strength and age; and with assiduous attention one should achieve the sweetening of the strident voice, which makes up the high tones; finally the whole register will become perfect in its total equalization. These advantages cannot be gained except through the most assiduous diligence, regulated by a solfeggio made up of notes of length, which ought to encircle

the low notes, pass to the middle of the voice, and finally
mingle with and unite the high voice. The union of these
voices should form a mixture so perfect as not to ruin the
union of the entire register. One cannot hope to obtain all
of this if he strays from the indicated rule, since only
through the calmness and spinning out of the voice can one
correct crudity and stridency. Once the scholar has arrived
at the possession of a happy and secure execution through
this method, he can extend those steps, which he will make
guided by wisdom and by the accuracy of his discernment, acquired through experience.

The other quality of voice which we have noted as defective but corrigible through study and art, is that of limited
register and somewhat weak. This type of voice is certainly
at a disadvantage, because it is only apt for use with good
effect in small places: a very notable disadvantage, since
necessity constrains us to sing now in large places, now in
small. One should not abandon absolutely such a voice, because we can be sure to be able to administer some help with
study, enough to render it richer and stronger. The greater
number of masters believe this defect can be corrected by
having the scholar sing every day in his lesson with a full
throat, hoping that the strength of this shouting and stridency will enable him to gain greater energy, and strengthen
the weak register. But this rule seems scabrous to me, because a student of twelve, thirteen or fourteen years cannot
have a chest strong enough to support such an unusual fatigue:
On the contrary, I am persuaded that this will ruin him entirely, or at least exhaust him, and weaken further whatever
small strength which he may have at such an age. As a matter
of fact I have never seen a good result from a similar method
of having a scholar sing with all his voice, even when he had
already developed the full robustness of his chest.

With a student of tender years one should never use vio-
lent remedies, but always the mildest and least dangerous.
Of all these my faithful master, Experience, has made me feel
one to be the best, which I here propose to you: Reflect. . .
a voice that is limited and weak, whether it be Soprano or
Contralto, will gain a not inconsiderable advantage, if in
its daily study it is cultivated with a solfeggio composed of
long notes; and the success will be even more secure, if this
same solfeggio does not exceed the range which its own nature
permits at this time. One must counsel the student to increase little by little the body of this type of voice, regulating it with the help of art, and continual exercise;
finally you will arrive at making it robust and sonorous.
This first obstacle overcome, one may change solfeggios,
which ought now to be augmented by notes a little higher; and

since this second portion of the voice belongs to the register of the head, as I have proved already, I shall speak in the following article of how to unite them: One cannot produce a good effect if the voice is not equalized and united in its whole range. With this continuous and well-regulated exercise, which should occur in the first years of every scholar, and with the aid of age, which carries with it the reinforcement of the chest and wisdom for guiding the studies well, he will certainly obtain that quantity of voice which will be sufficient for him to make himself heard in every place, no matter how vast.

I had experience of this remedy in a case followed carefully by me, one which I cannot ever forget, nor ever shall forget. Into my hands there came a youth who had been abandoned by two masters, otherwise very reputable, who firmly asserted that he did not have a good chest nor a good voice, and thus was useless to the art. I wished to examine him, for certain signs (signs which only the fine discernment of a practical Master can recognize) reveal an occult inclination regarding singing, and in my soul I have great hope in such happy concepts. I undertook voluntarily the fatigue and the work of exercising him, without fear of weakness and his tender age of thirteen: for a long space of time I never strengthened his voice; I paid attention only to perfect intonation, gradation and unification of his voice. With this method, after a certain determined time, I succeeded, with the growth of his years, in advancing him little by little in his studies to the point that he found his voice now florid, robust, and rich in its range, able to ascend with ease to high D-la-sol-re, and in consequence worthy to perform in any noble theater. I do not need to express the pleasure which I derived from this discovery of signs, and in this achievement. My dear Professors, do you not know the consolation we feel when a scholar succeeds in this manner?

It remains for me now to speak of those voices which are slender and weak throughout their register and which according to me, little selected, because every voice ought to have good body. One observes that these voices are very weak in the chest notes, and the greater majority deprived of any low notes, but rich in high notes, or head voice. If to this quality of voice one can procure an enlargement and strengthening of the unhappy little voice, it can become a good, pleasing and estimable voice. There is not method more sure to obtain this end, I believe, than to have such a little voice sing only in the chest voice for a time. The exercise should be done with a tranquil solfeggio; and as the voice enriches itself with greater body, and range, one may blend it as much as possible with the low notes, making the scholar understand at the same time that all of these voices should become not only sonorous and purged of all defects, but also expressive and vocalising with a rounded pronunciation, majestic in order to remove from them the childish pronunciation, which is alone innate in such little voices. Once such a difficulty is overcome, one can unite the rest of the voice, which makes up the register; and as much as this portion of the voice is of a favorable quality, so much will the union be easy and happy.

In the end it appears quite clear, that the rule of having the scholar sing full voice is not good in all cases, but on the other hand, I have said, in many cases it is prejudicial, especially when the scholar does not have a strong and firm voice. [B] It is certain in this case, that if he sings full voice, he cannot but increase his faults; should he sing sotto voce, he will himself remark even the smallest defect. This same moderate singing is the unique method for strengthening the voice, exercising it thusly with white notes. The master should not, therefore, permit the scholar to sing at full voice, until after he has obtained through age sufficient robustness of the chest, and then done it through study and long exercises to correct all his defects.

And now we must speak of the abuse of forcing the voice, before closing this article, Youths, I advise you to avoid an error into which from time to time even professors fall. When one has the chance to sing in a somewhat vast and full church, or theater, it often happens that a musician may have some doubts regarding the size of his voice. Such a one, because he has sung at a different time in the same place, which was almost empty, has heard his voice better, and it seemed to him to be more resonant, believes that the supposed exhaustion arises from other causes than the increased density of the air due to the quantity of people breathing, and from the loss of quiet through the murmuring of the people; and in order to better hear a strong repurcussion of his own voice in his own ear, he forces and sings with the whole throat. This is an error very prejudicial to the beauty of the voice, and to the strength of the chest. [C]

He who has once tested his voice, and through repeated experience has found it sufficient to be heard in whatever vast place, even though it seemed to him to be somewhat weak and exhausted; for him there is no need to force it, indeed he must ascertain that he is making the usual impression on the auditor. It is true, that the same quantity of voice is not sufficient for every place; and for this reason the great professor uses prior trials, reflections, and practice to know how to proportion his voice to every location: but it is also true, that when the professor does not find his voice

37

sufficient for a given vastness, he still should not force it, in order not to ruin the voice, and the chest. It remains only to decide that forcing the voice is one of the great errors which a singer can commit.

ARTICLE VIII: *OF THE UNION OF THE TWO REGISTERS, PORTAMENTO OF THE VOICE, AND OF THE APPOGGIATURA.*

Once the master, using the above described method, has strengthened and firmed up the voice of the scholar in whom it was weak and inconstant, he ought to have him pass to the study of the Portamento of the voice, and instruct him well therein, this being one of the principal parts of vocal singing.

I shall tell further on what I mean by the portamento of the voice.

It is enough to say here that such a portamento cannot be acquired by any scholar who has not already united the two registers, which are in everyone separated; in some a little, in some more.

I have already demonstrated sufficiently at another place what this separation is, and from what it emanates, and there indicated the easy manner of recognizing the note at which the two registers separate; I intend to tell how to teach the method which every scholar can use to tell for himself which note is the ultimate which he should give with the full strength of the chest, and what is the one which by precept belongs to the register of the head, or falsetto.

Nature is not the same in all persons, thus the separa-tion of the two registers will be in one person slight, and larger in another. It is a rare case when the two registers are both united into a chest register in one person. This total union is generally produced only by study and the help of art.

Even art and its helps will prove useless, if before all else the voice is not assigned its proper range, according to the best rules, regardless of the quality of the voice. For it has happened all too often that a good Soprano voice has been betrayed and by bad counsel tormented by being made to sing as a Contralto, and in reverse a perfect Contralto voice forced to sing Soprano. [A] And may God forgive the author of this misfortune! Students, beware of incorrect ranges, for then the rules of art will prove insufficient to produce a good effect; and on the contrary they will surely produce good effects, if the voice is correctly determined; and then the aids of art will work.

For example, take a scholar who has strengthened his chest tones, but has those of the head weak out of all pro-portion. In such a voice the separation of the two registers will reach from the soparno c-sol-fa-ut to the D-la-sol-re on the fifth line. (Soprano clef) Then suppose: the head voice being in need of help, since it is separated from the chest, the most certain method to help unite them is for the scholar, without losing time, to undertake to establish in his daily studies the manner of holding back the chest voice and of strengthening little by little the unfriendly notes of the head, in order to render the latter equal to the former in the best possible way. And it happens that this will distress the master no less than the scholar, because on the part of the scholar he must subdue a portion of the voice which is strong, and render vigorous another portion, which is by nature weak. On the part of the master it is necessary, after he has with ingenuity put the scholar firmly on this exercise, to hold him there, and to give him rules by which he can give strength back to the chest voice, so that he can check and see exactly what degree of strength has been attained by the unfriendly notes of the head. It may happen that the union of the two registers has not arrived at the desired point; nonetheless I beseech the master and the scholar not to lose courage thereby; because I am sure that, continuing the same way, they must have a happy success, and I add as much for the consolation of one as the other, that the scholar will learn insensibly how to take without pain and fatigue, the unfriendly notes which he is seeking. And in addition I predict that all other voices which follow this method, will strengthen themselves with equal vigor.

It is true that this effect comes later in a youthful chest. But it is also true that a youthful chest may learn it insensibly, whereas a more mature one requires more discernment to understand this rule well, and more strength in order to execute it.

This same rule ought to be used in the contrary case as well, that is to say, when the head voice is strong and the chest voice weak. With this one difference, that in the first case it was necessary to hold back the chest voice, and in this case it is necessary to hold back the head voice until they can both be united and equalized.

Arrived at this point and happy from the victory of the two voices united, the scholar can now turn his patient attention with less pain to the study which will produce the acquisition of the portamento of the voice, so necessary in every style of singing.

By this portamento of the voice is meant nothing but a passing, tying the voice, from one note to the next with perfect proportion and union, as much in ascending as descending. It will become more and more beautiful and perfected the less it is interrupted by taking breath, because it ought to be a just and limpid graduation, which should be maintained and tied in the passage from one note to another.

To enable the scholar to acquire easily this gift of

portamento of the voice, the best method is to make him exercise on a solfeggio sung with the two vowels A and E, so that
these become equally perfect.

But the proposed solfeggio ought to be written in white
notes, with forward motion and retrograde, and regular leaps
at the discretion of the writer. In the execution of this
solfeggio the scholar must abstain from taking breath on the
notes that rise in pitch, or that leap upward; but only take
breath on those which descend. [B]

In order that this very necessary rule to not take breath
does not seem too harsh and painful to the scholar, if he be
of a weak chest, it should be written with only two notes on
each beat, and let those be minims, so as to give the time a
slow movement, and give the voice adequate space for expand-
ing itself; and the scholar should not take breath between
the first and second notes, but only before beginning the
second beat. If the scholar should prove able to sustain
these two notes without pain, he may be permitted to pass to
the third, but not to more in order that he does not weaken
the chest. Thus, if one finds a scholar unusually robust of
chest, one should treat him in the same fashion as one with
a weak chest. To favor the robustness of this chest, one
should allow him to pass to other notes, and to breath accord-
ingly, only when mature age has rendered his organization
perfect and strong.

I shall tell the studious why it is that one prohibits
the scholar from taking breath when the voice rises in pitch,
and why one allows it in descending; here it is: to enrich
thereby and subdue that portion of the voice which one observes to be by nature the lazier and least apt to execution.
The masters of this beautiful art know that every voice as-
cends in pitch with difficulty: and is more free and open
in descending.

[C] Thus this rule serves to overcome the difficulty in
ascending, and demonstrates clearly the useful act in which
the scholar, according to a precept of the art, ought to take
the first note lightly little by little with his voice, and,
by another precept, pass without taking breath to take the
second note with the same gradation, to obtain a good effect;
and he will conserve the breath with such good economy that
in his progress he will accustom the bellows of the voice to
regulate, graduate and hold back the breath, and it will render him master of taking, re-taking and letting go of the
voice, and not to take the breath only following the necessity of insensible pain and fatigue.

I do not deny that this will cost him hard work at the
outset, but this hard work will put him in the state of singing with facility and pleasure in every kind of style; and

41

acquiring thus the robustness of the chest and facility in passing gradually from one note to another, he will see himself able to make an impasto of the voice so perfect that it will be said: "He sings to the heart."

Once the scholar has arrived at the level of sustaining and passing the notes as above without taking breath, he should continue his study, singing solfeggios of agility with the two vowels A and E, and this exercise will make him master of coloring at will any passage with that true expression which forms the cantilena colored with chiaroscuro, so necessary in every style for singing. With this same exercise acquiring little by little the studied art of graduating and sustaining the voice, he will find an easy facility in perfecting the messa di voce and he will fold up his breath with lightness; it is seen often to be interrupted, if in execution it is mixed up by excitement, or by an overlarge breath.

With the study of the portamento at an end, the scholar should apply himself to the appoggiatura, because there is no other thing which is more valuable joined to the former.

The appoggiatura is nothing but one or more notes held back. It is divided into simple and double, or gruppetto. The simple is when only one note has been held back. If this note has been held back in descending, it is called an appoggiatura from above, and should always be made up of a whole tone; if it is held back in ascending, it is called an appoggiatura from below, and should be composed of a single half tone. The double appoggiatura, or gruppetto, is when more have been held back; and this also has a place in ascending and descending; for this reason it is executed in two ways, as appear here in the example.

Both of these should end on the real note.

The value of the simple appoggiatura should be half of the note on which it falls; only if the note is of inequal value, the appoggiatura should be worth two-thirds. To execute them to perfection is truly not easy, because if they become overloaded in order to distinguish them, they escape the good order of proportion, and become in consequence crude and disgusting. The appoggiatura, the trill and the mordent are in reality only embellishments of song; but withal so necessary, that without them it becomes insipid and imperfect, since from these alone it acquires its highest prominence.

With all of this the scholar is advised not to use these except in cantilena and in suitable expressions, since these embellishments do not have a place everywhere; And far too many, ignoring these precepts, abuse them. To prove me right it is enough to go into the theater to hear a man or a woman, for example, in an aria of invective, singing with great fervor for the action, accompanying with an appoggiatura such words as *Tyrant, Cruel, Implacable,* and so forth, and ruining therewith the good order of the exclamation; I shall demonstrate this further on.

The rule which I have given, to not overload the appoggiatura, is not general, but is restricted solely to serious song. If he who sings in Buffo style emphasizes it, not only does he not commit an error, but he earns applause; because this same over-emphasis, which results in laughter in serious song, reaps approbation in Buffo style.

> And the sound of applause. . .with it
> Go vanquish the stars.

ARTICLE IX: *OF THE MESSA DI VOCE.*

[A] The graces of singing, which are those ornaments without which every song remains weak and tasteless, are: the appoggiatura, the messa di voce, the trill and the mordent. I have already discoursed on the appoggiatura in the preceding article; of the others I shall treat gradually in following articles; and in this one I shall speak of the messa di voce.

Messa di voce describes that action by which the professor gives to each long note a gradation, putting in it at the first a little voice, and then with proportion reinforcing it to the very strongest, finally taking it back with the same gradation as he used in swelling. [B]

Ordinarily this messa di voce should be used at the beginning of an aria, and on notes with hold signs; and similarly it is necessary at the beginning of a cadenza: but a true and worthy professor will use it on every long note, which are found scattered through every musical cantilena.

It is certain that the messa di voce lends great excellence to singing, as it renders it more pleasing to the ear, and if it be executed with perfection, and with the union of a trill, is enough to make a cadenza perfect, and I dare say also make a singer perfect in the sense that it enables him to sustain and graduate without any defect, and with facility his own voice, then he can hope to have come into possession of the secret no less than the art.

Truly the deceit of some modern virtuosi of singing is deplorable, when faced with the salutary effects which this exquisite rule produces, they disregard them and not only consider them useless, but like noxious things, commend them to exile and oblivion. They do not lack boldness, however, in order to be able to say they use this rule, and believe it enough to begin the messa di voce, and make the preparation alone, but their daring falls away soon enough when they see that the audience, hearing the forced voice, and above all else its ugly defective quality, becomes bored and writhingly tired of listening, since they do not find either art or gradation (faithful companion of the messa di voce) nor beginning, middle or end.

From one deceit pass to another, in which a few singers find themselves, who use the rule of the messa di voce, flattering themselves that they understand it. But in reality, in singing they demonstrate that they have not studied it.

These undertake the messa di voce by introducing a multiplicity of notes; but since they are ignorant of the manner of conserving the breath, and unable thereby to sustain them, must usually terminate the cadenza without a trill and are in consequence obligated to suppress the final note.

This, according to me, is a deceit of the most serious and unpardonable type, since it arises from lack of reflection, and temerity. If such a one had first examined himself and his forces well, and studied with care the rule I recommend, he would not certainly have undertaken to do that which he did, until he recognized that he was able to execute it with facility and security. But the abuse of over-reaching is so much introduced to the young of our day, that I cannot hope to extirpate it with my good advice.

I shall do everything, nonetheless, for the love of studious youths, to introduce the love of this exercise, and hatred for presumption, into their souls.

What the art is of strengthening the chest to make it able for every kind of singing, I have already taught in the preceding articles. Supposing that such strength of chest is acquired, it follows now that we should reason out the means which the scholar should use to attain the facility and perfection of the messa di voce.

I repeat that the scholar should not presume to be able to execute the messa di voce if he has not first acquired, in the manner described above, the art of conserving, reinforcing and taking back the breath: since on this alone depends the gift of the just and necessary gradation of the voice. Finding himself then in a state of sustaining long notes, the scholar should exercise himself in giving each note the gradation and the proportionate value which he can without great effort: [C] that is to say, from the beginning he gives a little voice, and proportionately reinforces it to that certain set grade from which he can diminish it with the same gradation which he adopted in swelling.

Do not doubt that in the beginning the scholar will find no little difficulty in the execution of the swell and diminish with equal gradation. But this difficulty will be in part reduced, if in doing the exercises he will fix the mouth well, as he should understand. The mouth should be scarcely open when starting the note, which helps the voice very much in coming forth sweetly, and then gradually it should be reinforced by opening the mouth until it reaches the limits prescribed by art. The scholar is advised to undertake the exercise of the messa di voce with moderation, because otherwise he will run the risk of tiring the chest, hence it will be best if at the beginning of this study, which should be daily without fail, he takes an occasional rest and relaxation.

I have gone far beyond the call of duty, reasoning so

45

much on the messa di voce, but I tell you, studious youths, that it is so close to my heart that I could speak of it forever. I conclude by placing before your eyes a cele- brated picture; I mean the estimable and valorous Don Carlo Broschi, commonly called Farinelli, who possessed the messa di voce, in addition to all other graces and ornaments of singing, to such perfection that common agreement, and my own, was that it was responsible for his immortal fame in singing.

Perhaps it would please you if I gave some resume of his life and worth, since he is such a worthy man, and such a dear friend.

Cavaliere Don Carlo Broschi was born in the Province of Bari, in the kingdom of Naples; without doubt he may be called the Baldassare Ferri of our century. As early as his first youth he was discovered to be furnished by nature with so many beneficial gifts, such as have been given to few, and one may say everything was given to him with a generous hand. His first studies were directed by the celebrated Niccolo Porpora, underwhom he made such rapid progress that in a short time his fame was known throughout Europe. His voice was considered surprising because perfect, strong, and sonorous in its quality, and rich in its range from the deepest low notes to the high, the equal of which has not been heard in our times. He was gifted also with a natural creativity which, led by wisdom, made strange things be heard, so individual that they left no room to others to be able to imitate them. The art of knowing how to conserve and take in breath with reserve and neatness, without ever becoming noticeable to anyone, began and ended with him; very perfect intonation, spinning out the voice and swelling the voice, his portamento, the unity, the surprising agility, his singing to the heart and his gracious manner, and a per- fect and rare trill, were all equal excellences in him; there was no style in the art which he did not execute with perfection and to such a sublime level as to remain inimi- table. As soon as the news went out, the theaters of the first cities of Italy fought to have him, and everywhere that he sang he reaped a merited applause to such extent that everyone spoke of him. Many courts of Europe did not delay in calling him, and he was everywhere admired, praised and well rewarded. This flourishing progress was in the first years of his youth. But our worthy man did not let this deter him from incessant study, until he succeeded in chang- ing in great part his first way of doing things, substituting a better one; and he undertook all of this in the period after he had already made his great name. Behold, dear read- er, a luminary and ornament of our profession, who was distinguished not only for the rarity of his talents, but admired as well for the wisdom of his conduct, for his warm heart which gave help to his friends, and benefited his enemies as well. He lives today in his country house near Bologna with that quiet provided by his retirement. If a man of such merit does not fail to study so assiduously, how much more should those others do, who are not gifted by nature with so many similar prerogatives.

ARTICLE X: *OF THE TRILL AND OF THE MORDENT.*

[A] Among the most necessary qualities, and beautiful embellishments of the art, with which every singer should be furnished, there is, it seems to me, no quality more interesting, nor embellishment sweeter than that which is commonly called the trill: when done this produces in the ears and in the souls of the audience the increase and the summit of tenderness, of pleasure and of love. Let a singer have a beautiful voice, let him have facile execution, and let him have good taste; nonetheless his singing, if not united to the sweet grace of a trill, will ever be imperfect, arid and dry. Put on display a professor who is industrious in joining together a good style, perfect cadenzas, perfect held notes, and the most perfect execution, but without a trill: display another, who lacks these qualities; but possesses alone a perfect portamento of the voice, method, understanding and direction of all of this, but who has a beautiful trill: ask the public to pass judgement on the two singers. Who can doubt it? The second, they say loudly, is preferred, pleases, is honored; because the perfection, the beauty and the final polish of singing is, in a word, the trill. To the voice of the public I add my own experimentation, and I assert that a cadenza composed of two notes alone, that is, a messa di voce. . .and a trill, is enough, and remains perfect, complete and believable; but if it has only an appoggiatura, if it races toward the final note without a trill, everything falls apart, and remains imperfect. [B] O trill! Sustenance, decoration, and life of singing! [C]
    And yet it is not without wonder, and horror, the clear evidence of these excellences and the indispensable necessity of the trill notwithstanding, that we see the trill in these days, I am constrained to say unhappy days, ignored and neglected. And who is to blame? Forgive me, honored masters of music, if a sincere voice speaks from my pen, but the guilt is not with the scholar. I know that the ordinary singer, not furnished with a trill, speaks of an ungrateful nature, which has not blessed him; but he is wrong; this is not a grace denied by nature; with easy study, patient and well regulated, it may be found in nature. But this is the place at which the master and the scholar must pool their resources. For if the first does not find in the second a natural disposition, and a strong ability to overcome the indispensable obstacles for the acquisition of a perfect trill, he is annoyed, his interest lags, and he loses his effect on the scholar; the latter, intimidated from singing by the other, and humiliated by the screams of the impatient

48

master, loses his application, and little by little even
his desire, and finally despairing of reaching a happy result, tired out, seeks all the possible ways to avoid and
abandon this study. How well I know this, that it is possible, and I pray the one and the other to not lose their
enthusiasm, and run to those extremes which are so prejudicial to both alike. No art teaches itself; none can be
learned without an infinite tolerant patience.

At this point I see the question which you wish to ask,
that is, whether I can give a certain rule to form a system
for directing and regulating a scholar who wishes to possess
himself of the trill. I answer, what can I say? I confess
that this certain rule cannot be found at this moment in the
author. In order not to let you think that my other reflections are fraudulent, I shall say that in many cases I have
seen voices so agile that they could execute every other
passage, in every other style, and of the most difficult
type; passages [D] that even resembled trills; [E] and on
the contrary I have observed voices of mediocre quality, which
yet had a trill. So I shall give you here the rules given by
an author of no small repute, Pierfrancesco Tosi: this most
honored man said, that if a master wished to carry out his
obligations in teaching, he should use vocal, speculative
and instrumental examples, to help his student to acquire
the trill. . .equal, beaten, solid, easy, and moderately
fast: which are precisely the qualities the most beautiful
and often remarked by all the authors, and by the common
experience of the profession.

By universal common law the trill is always composed of
a true note, a real note, with the addition of a false one.
It should always begin on the false note, and always finish
on the true note. The false note should always be a whole
tone above the true one, and the two should be equally
vibrated. [F]

Although this trill is effective by itself, by reason of
its multitude of figurations and varied positions, has come
to be commonly divided into eight different species. Exactly
thus did the above-cited Pierfrancesco Tosi divide it in his
Chapter on the Trill at page 24, where he not only distinguished each species with practical reasoning arising from
the art itself as indubitably executed by the most worthy
professors, but for greater clarity he gave to each species
its distinct name. He discoursed with such accuracy on these
eight species of trill, that I can do no more than repeat
the same, if I wish to speak clearly on the subject.

I do not wish to repeat for the scholar everything
written by Tosi: so I shall speak only of the three most
difficult species of trill, giving my thoughts on what should

be their true and just execution.

Of these three species, the first is called the increased (*cresciuto*) [G] trill, because it should rise in pitch. The second is called the diminished trill, (*calato*) [H] because it should descend; of these two, both should have a precise and distinct gradation. This point is among the most difficult of the art, because it is so necessary in ascending and descending, that the singer know the art of sustaining and managing the breath, because he must not interrupt the scale in ascending nor descending; and he ought to be able to pass from one trill to another with pure and secure proportion so that the voice makes no change, but passes exactly from one tone to another in ascending and descending.

These two scale-trills, made according to true art, will certainly bring great praise and honor to the perfect executor; but it will cost him great fatigue and time to be able to reduce the fullness of his voice to easy execution.

The third species has been called the redoubled trill; this duplication, executed with just proportion and with the art of sustaining with the breath, and that reinforcement and diminution of the voice, necessary to give it its proper form, is enough by itself; although performed without any other passage, let it be prepared by a held note, or a fermata, and its sole simplicity will procure applause and honor. Let us illustrate this doctrine with an example.

Imagine the note C-sol-fa-ut of the soprano, situated on the fourth space. One begins this C-sol-fa-ut with a messa di voce, which should be held to that perfect gradation prescribed by art, then the voice returns to its former level of volume, and the trill should be begun on the designated note as shown here. [I]

messa di voce. Trillo raddoppiato

The first note above should form a messa di voce; the other which follows, is that upon which the first trill is made; and immediately after that the other three notes which one takes for passing again to the trill: but these must be taken in the same breath, without dividing them in any manner with the voice, but with a light and tied motion the note of the next trill is taken. [J]

This point of the art will be excellent every time it is

executed to perfection, but it is necessary therefore not to undertake it blind, nor without first making an advance study, mature and solid.

A good chest is necessary to sustain the first note; art in order to know how to conserve the breath; and mature judgement in order to know how to allot the value of the messa di voce to retain enough strength to bring the redoubled trill to a perfect end. In sum I judge that he who lacks natural and artistic gifts, should not undertake the redoubled trill, since the execution will be without doubt unhappy.

The mordent is born from the trill. This differs from the trill, because the trill, as I have said, is composed of one real note and a real and equal vibration with another note a tone above; and the mordent is composed of a true note with the beating of another false note a half-tone below, and this false note should be struck more slowly and with less strength and less value than the real note, but even so the mordent, like the trill, should always end equally.

The mordent has the singular advantage of being able to blend anywhere in the art, and is apt for any style of singing; therefore any time that it can be put in its proportionate niche, it is just to use it. He whose fate it is to acquire the trill, let him hope to acquire the mordent as well; and I assure him that although the mordent ought to be closer and faster than the trill, the scholar will acquire it easily if he will exercise often on a solfeggio of agility, with notes fixed in various places; [K] and it will begin to form without pain and anxiety this amiable grace, the mordent, which will always prove pleasing and grateful equally with the trill, when the one and the other are made without defect, without blot and shall be perfect.

It remains for me to speak here of the perfection and the defects of the mordent and the trill in this last part, as the last passage of the love which I have already demonstrated for studious youth in all my reasoned plans. Of perfection I have already spoken above in mentioning Tosi. Here I shall speak of defects.

Among trills the most defective are: the goat-bleat, and the horse whinney. Both are committed through the errors of capricious youths, heedless of the counsels of their masters; because of this they forget the infallible rule for beating the trill, sustaining the breath and upset the light action of the fauces, by means of which they reduce the just perfection of the trill. Everyone will understand therefore, and recognize the origins of the goat-bleat and horse-whinney trills, and the reason why they carry these names, placed upon them by professors: I wish to say that it is

51

because the singer does not avail himself of the motion of the fauces, but only of the motion of the mouth, and that in the manner and guise which he uses when he laughs, so that consequently he makes a natural sound like the bleating of a goat or the whinneying of a horse. The defects of the trill are not limited to the two mentioned above; there are many others. Some who do not have these faults form horrid trills, unpleasing in the extreme, because they sustain the trill with a slow motion; because they rush over a good beginning; because they change the motion, now at the middle, some leave go of it when they have just begun it, and others, who begin it, never let it go. [L]

Wisely then the master, after having explained to his scholar in what method the trill should be formed, will exercise him therein, content at the first with movement that is slow and languid which is all that puerile age supplies the youth, and will demonstrate that he is content and satisfied; thus in going along encouraging the youth, and strengthening his voice, he will form a vigorous and robust trill. I praise the diligence, love and art of the professor who never humiliates his loving scholars. And I praise the diligence of those scholars who, knowing that they have trills of bad quality, are not content with the counsels of the master, but by themselves go to hear worthy singers, industriously studying them in order to imitate; no, there is no shame nor wickedness in copying the good and the beautiful in all the arts of worthy men.

Now that the youth has in some way possessed himself of a trill of noble quality, he ought to study how to avail himself of it with wisdom and judgement; and at the right place; it is bad if the trill is not well situated; worse if the scholar makes too much show of it; otherwise he will annoy infinitely, and prejudice thereby the merits of his own singing. [M] For example, if he mingles it with the tempo of a siciliana, he will get the worst effect, because the movement of this tempo requires portamento, and legato of the voice; and the trill will make a caricature of the tempo.

But should I always be on the side of the scholars? and never bow with respect to the professors? Most worthy masters, you, more than I know, see the necessity which the singer has for this divine trill, without which every cadenza remains imperfect and languishes. You know that a trill should be placed on a convenient note; a note which needs to be vibrated, however cantabile the cantilena may be; because otherwise the passage remains flaccid and languid; and flaccid and languid the gruppetto which follows. [N]

Reflect then, that all the strength of this study should

be regulated by art and by reason, which will give a just
and pleasing division; praise that virtuoso who, in the place
where the word and the music cry for a trill, gives a trill
and not an appoggiatura; and where an appoggiatura is required, gives that and not a trill, for infallibly the result
will be of the best. In sum I say everything in one word,
that all strength rests in perfect judgement, and understanding of the use of the graces of the art, which are in sub-
stance themselves the beauty of the art and the formation
of the virtuoso style, which distinguishes the professor
from the mediocre and the best; avail yourselves of these
graces in appropriate time and place, I say.

ARTICLE XI: *OF CADENZAS.*

Because I have already spoken of the messa di voce and trill in two other articles, some will believe that this one, dealing with cadenzas, is entirely useless. [A] I know that these are of the opinion that in order to close a cadenza perfectly it is sufficient to have a mass of notes circulating from the lower notes through the middle to the acute; and enough to finally bring it to an end with a single trill. I also know that these same persons suppose that there is nothing easier in the whole art, than the making of a cadenza. Yes, I have noted that many think thus, but I know better, that they deceive themselves greatly: and I do not shiver to assert that the cadenza is usually a part of the most scabrous and thorny problems of vocal music; because it is necessary to overcome many difficulties in order to arrive at forming it perfectly.

To know that I speak the truth, it is enough to know how many things are required to perfect a cadenza. All of these necessary things I will here explain exactly to you.

First: it must be free and secure in modulation; without this freedom one runs risk of beginning the trill in another key. Second: it is necessary to know how to rule and measure the breath. Third: it would be a great advantage to be gifted with a creative mind (and these are the traits of the unexpected genius, improvised, parts of the creative mind, which suddenly distinguish a man, and carry him to the stars with acclaim). And for this one must have a straightforward judgement, which is necessary to regulate every note to its perfection.

All of these necessary qualities can be acquired by anyone in some degree with study. Even though the creative mind is ordinarily a pure gift of the beautiful nature; yet, attacking with study, one can acquire it to such a degree that one who achieves it by study may be considered as a paragon, even when compared with one who has it as a gift of nature.

The art of knowing how to sustain and measure the breath, to rule with just proportion the cadenza from beginning to end, in order not to be constrained to interrupt it, is one of the principal and most necessary treasures which the scholar can win.

I add the necessity for correct judgement in this way because that is what should guide one to the knowledge of himself, so that he undertakes only that which he is capable of doing with security, and can escape the embarrassment occassioned by shortness of breath; and this same error is not alone, for one may find himself not only in the state of being unable to perfect the cadenza with a trill, but also unable to make the final note heard; this same judgement should lead the singer to choose a motive from the cantilena of the music of the aria, and words which are in the same style of tenderness, love, or whatever they should be, and not betray them with a cadenza which belongs to an agitated aria; and in diverse other passions, opposed, as one might do in allegro style, bringing in a cadenza appropriate to the aria which says "Parto ma tu ben mio, etc." All of these things happen, and you see it is because the cadenza is not regulated by judgement, but by caprice alone, and by a voluntary negligence.

This is the place for the question of whether they are wise who believe that they acquire good names and credit by drawing out a cadenza to great length.

I say that those who do not exceed beyond a certain point may well be called judicious; but regulated by wisdom, and art, lead the cadenza to an end without ever going beyond those limits which are sure to annoy. He who undertakes too much encounters frequent obstacles, and in order to overcome them with an easy remedy, abandons the gradation and just expression, and takes refuge in a multiplicity of notes, which not being sustained according to the rules of art, are heard to be sliding around and repeating the passages already sung. Here is the way in which a worthy man, who is constrained to execute a cadenza together with some instruments, either wind or string, will never overstep the limits nor exceed just and convenient measure: That which is good, united to proportionate brevity will procure for him who uses it, universal esteem. Since the voice will be completely isolated from the first note to the last note of the cadenza, he should purge it of every small defect: the intonation, which makes the first figure, should be sustained in its exact center, since the gradation, the expression and the strength are joined to it, by means of which the needed regulation of the voice gives that brio which of necessity should distinguish each note to its final point, and should above all make the last syllable of every word heard, without being languid and dead.

Everything so far explained is without doubt necessary for bringing a good cadenza to a fitting close, and everything else which may be required rests with the good judgement of the good executor; and he who knows enough to take a motive or a passage from the body of the ritornello of the aria, and blend it judiciously with the rest of his invention, will reap particular applause. The studious youth can, by constant application, easily come into possession of this

55

so advantageous gift, and ought to regard it as a precept of the art itself. Is it then easy, or difficult to possess oneself of the above named gifts? Certainly I should confess with all frankness that it is consummately difficult; and for this reason, those who wish to succeed should not spare fatigue nor attention in order to understand well the instructions of great masters, and follow the examples of the best professors.

Every scholar then, who has arrived at the end of sustaining his voice, should not neglect, by means of the wise counsels of his master, to begin to exercise at beginning his cadenza, which however should at first be made up of but a few notes, the exercise thus begun will provide little by little the means whereby he can take command, and will render him capable, with the increase of his strength, and his art, of continual growth in length and ability to form it perfectly. The cadenza is necessary to every appropriate finale, and whatever the aria or other, if it be written by a master with art, wisdom and taste, if a cadenza be not made by the singer, the whole remains imperfect and languid.

The master should certainly oblige the scholar to be obedient to his own time; but he should also be discreet in pretending that this alone will not harm the voice, or that weaken the chest, and ought to content himself with that little which is enough to enable the singer to accustom himself to unite a cadenza with a trill, as is suitable to his age and his strength. They use different methods in other schools, not permitting the scholar to undertake to make a cadenza, if he has not reached a certain age which they call suitable, for they believe him unable to do it before without prejudicing the chest. This delay carries with it a major disadvantage to the scholar; and thus even greater damage and error in permitting him to take breath more often, because he finishes the cadenza in pieces, and flat on his face. This they call the expedient of art, but in reality it is a thing opposed to all the rules, which tell us otherwise. The best method, and the true expedient is this, which I have proposed before: the student should begin to accustom himself at the right time to make cadenzas; let them not be more than he can do without pain, and in this way he will succeed; one solidifies each time in this way, until he has acquired suitable strength; and then going ahead with the above-mentioned exercises to acquire strength, and proportionately he will go always forward.

Whoever follows the proposed rules can be sure of not erring; indeed, I believe, he will surely succeed with them. In every art he who adapts himself for a time to being able to perform that which is advisable, achieves thereby some progress, and an almost certain success; thus let all be guided by customary caution, and judgement, and regulated by a wise master, to whom the scholar should be blindly obediant and never depart from his good advice.

[A] The reflections which I have already set forth are all adaptable to every type of voice, and to every chest. [B] *Intonation, The Union of the Two Registers, The Messa di voce, The Appoggiatura, The Portamento, The Trill, The Mordent and The Cadenza*, can all be executed by every singer, and should be; since, when nature has not granted him these gifts, he can achieve them through study and art.

Agility of voice alone is such a very unusual gift of nature that one to whom it is denied, cannot hope to acquire it in any manner.

It is true that in our day we do not lack, without doing injustice to any of our presumptuous singers, for those who believe that they have this agility of the voice. But from the discomfort with which they execute it, they clearly demonstrate that they are lacking this gift.

My intention is to demonstrate from whence comes this confusion, and how it can be removed from our profession.

I confess that after many serious reflections on this point, I have not found anything else which I can say to you except that it is a false opinion which many singers hold, that they cannot please or win merit unless they sing with agility; and for the sake of avid applause they force themselves to sing agility in any way then can: or it may arise from the bad method of those masters, who although they find no natural disposition in the scholar, still oblige him to sing agility, and give him all the precepts, which form in him a habit of execution, or even a firm though false, belief that he possesses agility perfectly. But those deceive themselves in their opinion, and these in their method. Those, because it is false, as I have said in another article, that it is agility alone which is the excellence of the voice which renders the singer worthy of esteem and honors: These because it is impossible that a scholar, who has a heavy and crude voice, can with study alone make it perfectly agile and smooth.

The agility of the voice cannot be perfect if it is not natural; and if it is not perfect, instead of bringing pleasure and delight to the listener, it will bring annoyance and boredom.

Then he who does not have it from nature should never lose time vainly in trying to acquire it, nor put out the effort and the breath in seeking to execute it, thus the prudent master, finding the scholar to lack a natural disposition for singing agility, should cease to conduct him by this route, but lead him to another, since in this profession the ways are many, the styles are varied, as are the dispositions by which one may arrive at the desired honor of being a good and admired virtuoso.

If, however, the expert master recognizes a slight disposition to singing agility in his student, he should firmly place him on the road which will enable him to extend his ability, and thus amplify his style, which is already being formed. [C] Great attention should be paid during this study, in order not to enervate the strength of the chest of the scholar, nor to overload him with exorbitant burdens, nor to have him undertake (whenever the solfeggio is in a vivacious tempo) to perform it in the same motion, which the accompanying Cantilena employs. The surest means is to have him vocalize with distinctness, composure, so that every note is correctly in tune and purged of every defect.

This regulated study should be indispensably shaped to the ability of the age and the strength of each scholar, and after he has acquired the most robustness, the master should imperceptibly increase the time which regulates the measure in which the effect is produced, that in progressing thus he may free the voice to the point that he may lead it to true velocity in the motion, as we have found this by experience, to work.

It has been observed, and still is observed, that benign nature liberally conceeds to some an agility of execution so happy, that without any study everything they undertake is easy for them. This extraordinary gift, if followed according to the rules of art and a pure modulation, not only ought to bring praise, but also admiration. The ground will fall from under those who, enriched by their natural prosperity, pay little attention to any other, which is needed to unite a perfect and varigated style, without reflection, conserving constantly this sole manner of singing, not thinking that the advance of age will be to their great detriment, because as the chest loses its first strength, they will not only find themselves unable to proceed with this style; but incapable of taking up another method as well. The master should then think for a time on all of this, and encountering a similar ability should not neglect that good beginning so that the scholar makes a customary and regulated study, through which means he can avail himself of another system, should he lose the strength for agility. There are many who believe themselves to sing agility well, because out of four notes they make the first and last heard, while the others are silent. This should truly not be called agility, but rather an irregular undertaking contrary to the laws of art. [L] On the other hand, there are those who believe they will win esteem by beating all the notes with unmeasured strength, and inequality of voice, but rather cast into oblivion that just gradation, and paste-like quality which ought necessarily to be united to form a perfect execution; finally others have been observed which beside the above-named defects use a movement of the tongue, believing this makes the execution easier. [L] Every scholar should therefore know, that he not err, that the beauty of every kind of passage, and to well-execute one, consists in its being in tune, that its execution should be produced by the lightness of the fauces, accompanied and sustained by the robustness of the chest. Thus made, every note will be heard, he will know how to make it distinct and vibrant, if the cantilena of the passage requires it, and thus equalising the voice, he can proceed to greater speed, and will render himself the possessor of that other gift of coloring every passage with piano and forte so necessary to give it its just gradation and expression.

The master must never set his student on the path of this study unless he has first perfectly united the two registers of the voice, as I outlined in Article VIII, because otherwise their disparity will be easily heard.

One should pay attention also to acquiring by means of study, of which I have treated in the preceding articles, the art of conserving and taking back the breath, because without this one cannot ever execute well any kind of agility. In conclusion, he who wishes securely and promptly to acquire the above-mentioned agility ought with assiduous attention to exercise on vocalises. If the scholar remembers to begin the vowels perfectly, then the beauty of every passage will not be prejudiced; and if the vowel E is not begun on its true place, it runs the risk of being ridiculously taken for I and U. I call it ridiculous, because generally passages do not come out well if they are taken on the vowels I, O, and U, which with another name, our profession calls "prohibited;" on the other hand I counsel the scholar to accustom himself to vocalising with these as well, because sometimes the necessity arises of having to pronounce a passage on these as well, and specially on O; because these cases are rare, the scholar should practice more often on A and E.

The worthy master should guide his scholars on the right way, so that he may perfect himself in this very difficult style; let him who possesses a perfect trill not be miserly in mixing appropriately on every note where it will give prominence and bravura; thus also he should use the mordent in suitable places, and avail himself of the infinite vibration and vitality; and further in the tempo of the siciliana he will find it useful to mix the slide [*scivolo*] and the

down-slide [*strascino*], as long as they are placed in suitable positions and given with the just proportion. He should
also always sustain the voice in its proper pitch, because by
abandoning it he gives up one of the great excellences; and
he must also take heed of the just proportion, regulating
the high notes with sweetness and facility, removing every
portion of crudeness, which offends the listener; such a
method of execution ought to carry the student without doubt
to that true perfection which he should always desire. I
have already spoken of the natural agility, and should now
pass to a discussion of the other types, which one can mix
with this kind of agility.

The first type is generally called hammered [*martellato*]
[D]. This consists in beating every note the same. The
voice beats the same note several times, and of the four, the
first ought to be higher than the other three written on the
same line.

This type of agility is very difficult to execute to
perfection, because to make a success one must have a very
agile voice, a particular talent for applying oneself, and
indefatigable study.

In every case, before undertaking this study, it is
necessary to have the art of perfectly ruling the breath, of
being able to detach it and take it back without fatigue;
one must have the purest intonation, so that every hammered
note is distinctly in tune. These notes should be lightly
distinct, and reinforced only where the cantilena requires
it, or they overlap into caricature, rendering the cantilena
similar to the song of a broody hen, which screams and
deafens, happy to have laid an egg.

This style of agility is practically out of use today
because of the difficulty of its execution.

The last professors who used this hammered agility with
facility and mastery were [E] Agostino Fontana, scholar of
Antonio Pasi, and la Viscontina, of Milan.

After these two I have not heard another voice which has
perfectly executed this style of hammered agility, and I fear
that our profession will never acquire another if the new
scholars, after having received from nature the enumerated
gifts, do not apply themselves to the effort of a very long
and diligent study. [F]

The other style of agility is called singing by leaps
[*sbalzar*], [G] and is formed of notes of long value or of
less value, and is always a most difficult style of agility
singing, and difficult to acquire.

The master should therefore examine the scholar first
and see if he can succeed, since if he does not know that
he is able, he should neither force him nor oblige him to

study it, but rather content himself with exercising in the other natural method, which may be more successful, without making him lose time uselessly. In the already proposed method of singing, to be well-learned, one must have a robust voice, sonorous, agile and rich with profound low notes and high notes, and it should usually be a soprano voice; he who does not find all of these prerogatives united in himself should absolutely not undertake to learn this style.

Singing by leaps requires a particular study, totally separated from all the others. Intonation, for example, however perfectly rendered in other methods, in this one must be studied anew to accustom the voice to leap from the lowest to the highest, intoning each perfectly.

This is believed by some to be quite easy, but it is not in reality, because beside leaping with perfect intonation it is necessary to give a balanced measure to the voice as much in leaping up as in leaping down; it is natural, that in themselves the lower notes are more vibrant, or sustained by strength according to need, and yet the high notes, however they be used, should always be treated with sweetness, thus there should always be conserved a correspondent proportion between the one and the other. It is also necessary that perfect execution be united to a portamento of the voice, since if this does not bind the first note to the second, one will hear that detachment which belongs only to those who sing the bass, or to that buffo who reaps laughter and applause with his leaps and caricatures; detached notes are also permitted to the serious singer, if he makes them where they are appropriate, for instance to vivify the end of a passage, or if he wishes to highlight a proportionate place, which he deems convenient.

In this style of singing, as I have inculcated in all the others, the most necessary thing for success, is the art of knowing how to conserve the breath, and manage it. In order to arrive at the possession of the knowledge of singing by leaps, the most sure study is to begin to leap with the voice on long notes, and these very well in tune, holding the voice and passing a number of notes without taking breath, with caution always to not force them, in order not to prejudice the chest.

This method will facilitate for the scholar the execution of passing to another study on notes of lesser value, the stabilized intonation from the above exercise, and the art of knowing how to conserve the breath will facilitate his learning this other style which is faster, and consequently more difficult.

The solfeggio should not be made only with regular leaps but also mixed with irregular ones, so that the scholar should never encounter by chance any thing which would embarass him. One should finally examine what rule the scholar should follow, in exercising by leaps from low to high, that he may reap a sure profit. If the master should wish to follow this method, which is recognized by the best schools to be profitable, he should tell the scholar that the first note, being situated low, and the second high, he ought to take the last note with an appoggiatura vibrated from below. [H]

But given the case that the appoggiatura from below on the second note mentioned above, is not admitted, what effect results? According to my weak understanding, the result cannot be but bad, because if this style of singing will come to be called bravura, taking the second note without a vibrant appoggiatura makes it lose immediately its natural value, which is so necessary for this style of singing; in fact, by trying to prove it, everyone will see that what I have said is more than true: I am certain that it has been the custom, and still is the custom, in a cantabile aria, to hold in proportionate time the voice on a low note, and to pass to a high one, take this high one with an appoggiatura; but it is also certain, that it will remain less noticeable, as the motion of the leap becomes slower. On the other hand one observes that in the same cantabile style, having taken the low note, to pass to the following, the seventh or octave of the first, by not using the appoggiatura, but taking the note which forms the seventh or octave with the voice tied, without taking breath, one achieves a brilliant result. [I]

[J] This method, however, cannot be called bravura, but rather legato singing, and carried, which when well-executed and appropriate, produces universal approbation.

[K] Up to now we have reasoned on all the rules of the art; in the following articles let us reason on the studies, which a youth ought to make before he presents himself and his art of singing to the public.

To conclude this article, it pleases me to demonstrate to studious youths a proof of sincere love; and this advice I give as it was given to me by one of my worthy and loving masters, as a pledge and memory of the affection with which he taught me; and for his sake I have kept it always alive in my heart. Be advised, youth, to never be timid, nor flaccid, nor fearful when you wish to sing to the public; you must have spirit, spirit, courage, animosity; otherwise everything will end badly, languidly, and contemptibly.

I know that timidity is natural to beginners; thus a dextrous master will cure it when he finds a scholar able to sing in public, by producing him a little at a time; first before confidants and friends, and then adding a few more, and more important.

63

But note well that I said spirit and spirit, but I did not mean impudence and temerity. Modesty, gifts and nature and study, united in a worthy singer, will secure the admiration of the public, and garner firm and enduring applause.

In singing do not neglect to be constantly aware of what you are doing; do not wander, nor be distracted, or be of ill-will; even so, man is not always of the same disposition, and desire; but now happy, now melancholy and sad; in such a case, let the youth overcome his natural disposition, in which he finds himself, since he goes that day to sing to the public, and be firm with himself, making himself happy, joyful through virtue, if not at that moment through nature: like disinclination, annoyance is one thing which gives birth to, and produces, languid singing, and disgusting, so that the listener says: "When will this aria finish?" Thus happiness, spirit and vivacity produce happy singing, suave and rewarding to the ears of the hearers, in such a way that the singer and the listener are both content; and if he hears a da capo, he listens. But the greatest source of this happiness and vivacity in a singer lies in rendering execution easy to himself, and here is the most evident reason, since in this case the professor, having gathered all his thoughts and having the happy wish to sing, promises us that he is anticipating the following song with all his mind, and this is that famous foresight which prepares him for execution, and which renders it easier for him, and more beautiful, grateful and rewarding to the listener.

ARTICLE XIII: *OF THE KNOWLEDGE WHICH ONE SHOULD HAVE IF HE WISHES TO RECITE WELL IN THE THEATER.*

As I have already said, it is not only beauty and agility of voice which distinguishes with singularity the virtuoso, but also an excellent method of reciting which he should be able to produce, and which will win approbation and great reward.

When an actor recites well, investing strongly the character of the personage he is representing, and sets him forth naturally and with actions, and the voice, and the proper gestures, and brings him to life with clarity, the listener will say that he is truly, for example, Caesar: or that one is Alexander.

Now an actor cannot express naturally these gestures, nor make the effects clearly understood to the audience, if he does not understand the strength of words; if he does not know the true character of the person that he represents; and if he does not have a good Tuscan pronunciation. [A]

To acquire these diverse understandings, three different studies must be undertaken by the actor; that is, the Latin language [B]; history; and the Italian language.

The virtue and the strength of a word are not always revealed in its nature alone, but often in the manner, with which they are pronounced, whence they gain strength: this manner of pronunciation is learned from the study of Grammar. In fact, as one writes, so should he speak; and since he who reads cannot understand, or can easily deceive himself of the true sense of a writing without commas or periods: thus one who hears someone discoursing, and never hears an interruption, nor a change in the tone of the voice, cannot understand well. Grammar teaches the regulated way of writing, reading and speaking.

Listen to the discourse of a good orator, and hear what pauses, what variety of voice, what diverse strength he adopts to express his ideas; now he raises the voice, now drops it, now he quickens the voice, now harshens, now makes it sweet, according to the diverse passions which he intends to arouse in the listeners. Since the rules of grammar are only theoretical, one should learn the habit of reading Tuscan books, and listening to Italian orators. Reading pleases me, when one is alone in one's room with a good book, expecially of poetry, reading aloud, which is a useful exercise, and is an easy means of arriving at discoursing with just interruptions and changes of the voice: in consequence of which, one recites well in public.

The study of grammar should be followed by that of sacred,

profane, and fabulous history. You will find that virtuosi, who truly do not pass their days in idleness, are busy with some reading, reading the origins of nations, the changes, the revolutions of emperors, the wars, the truces, the following peaces, and such things: this knowledge is useful to him for pleasure, and for ornament, but I do not mean to tell you that it is as necessary to him as to the actor. It is enough for him, who is, being a virtuoso, a voyager, very sufficient if he know the virtue and the predominant passions of a nation; he should know the common means of conversing, use of clothing, and such things in sum, which characterize and distinguish one nation from another, among which he may find himself by chance.

But history is an indispensable necessity to an actor; it is sacred, profane and fabulous.

Suppose an actor wishes to represent for example, Julius Caesar in the scene in the senate, where surrounded by the traitorous conspirators, he is assaulted. . .would it not be a ridiculous thing if he did not know how to dress himself with the strength of soul of such a hero; and instead of sustaining the assault with presence and intrepidity of spirit, he let it be seen on the contrary as acts of fear, flight and villany?

Would it not be a ridiculous thing if, in a scene from a fabulous drama, composed of Mercury on the one hand, on the other Neptune, and the latter taken by an actor who treated it with acts of agility, vivacity and spirit, when it should have actions, movements and manners of an old man?

Would it not be a ridiculous thing, in a sacred drama representing the famous sacrifice of Abraham, if the actor held his knife trembling, this most obedient patriarch, and let resistence and tears figure in his religious resignation of Isaac?

Yet all of these may come to pass if the actor has not the first idea of history.

It remains to say a few things about the two languages, Latin and Italian; of the first I will not speak, since every virtuoso knows how necessary it is to singing in church, to know how to distinguish the long from the short; and also because the scope of my articles is completely directed to the theatrical singer.

That the Italian language is, above all, the most harmonious, the sweetest, the most suave for adapting itself to good music, every nation must confess, whether it wishes or not. Read the letter of Monsieur Rousseau, written "On the French Music," and you will see that I speak the truth; and the author is French. He means by this that the Italian language is the purest and most perfect language; as one should say,

66

the Florentine tongue in a Sienese mouth, with the grace of a Pistoian.

All the other Italian languages have defects in the theater. These similarly defective languages lack that melody and sweetness which the pure language has by grace of its accents: they are thus incompatible with good music, for their vowels are cut short of having a neat, well-bred and decisive sound, being instead a species of diphthongs, a coming together of two diverse sounds, which is after all the great reason why the French language is so little appropriate to music.

However, not all those who follow the profession of singing can be Tuscans, and the larger part of the professors are not, since this choice is freely open to all the nations and provinces which make up beautiful Italy, the Bolognese, Modenese, Milanese, Venetians and wise Neapolitans. These learn the true tongue from their masters, which they have not learned as students, and they often learn it better than those same Florentines, who have difficulty ridding themselves of a tendency of their area to speak in the throat. [C]

But believe me, there are two methods which are better than any master, as I propose, and they are efficacious and valid for making one learn the true language.

First: A youth, dedicated to the profession, in my judgment should sojourn a few years in Tuscany, as many have done, and I did myself: Youth in conversing inhales the pronunciation insensibly, as a child its milk, without school, without study, without art, for in this house nature itself is master, and age; but since not all can do this, for various reasons, I suggest this other, which is the reading of books, and conversation with men of pure pronunciation and good language.

And there, succinctly set down, are the three most valid means for correcting a bad pronunciation and a bad accent. How much a perfect pronunciation, a perfect accent, and a perfect sense of the words are necessary to a singer, has been demonstrated for us by the example of all those worthy professors listed by me in the second Article. These were for the most part Neapolitans, Bolognese and Lombards, and I know that there was no theater in any nation, or country, where they were taken for anything but Tuscans.

The divine Demosthenes recognized this excellence in an actor as well; and he knew how prejudicial defective pronunciation is to those who wish to perorate and declaim in public, for which he was often acclaimed the first orator of Greece, and knwoing himself in reality to be such, this great man feared that the defect of his tongue could easily cause him to lose the name, fame and universal esteem of his and other nations; thus in infinite discomfort he declaimed in a

67

loud voice in solitary places, holding in his mouth tiny pebbles, to loosen the natural tightness of his tongue; thus he exhorts us to quietly remove our defects, at whatever cost.

I hope that the examples given have persuaded my youthful lovers of vocal music to spare no travail nor effort to render themselves able in this area, which I value so much, since it seems to me to be that which renders every cantilena graceful and pleasant.

ARTICLE XIV: *OF RECITATIVE AND ACTION.*

When the studies of the Latin and Italian languages are
completed and finished with profit; and that of history;
studies so necessary for good recitation, as I have said,
the scholar can undertake with courage the study of the art
of acting.

I do not know why so few students count this art for so
little in our day, as it has fallen from its high level of
splendor and excellence in which it was held thirty years ago.

A great part of our actors believe that they have sufficiently discharged their duty in the theater when they sing
perfectly the arias alone, when neither the cantilena nor the
recitative is accompanied by suitable action. Another portion
recognize the necessity for good recitation, and good action,
but they excuse themselves with colorful pretexts, charging
the modern writers, saying that it is impossible to declaim
the recitatives which are written in our times, because they
are interrupted and the true sense of the words is upset by
the constant movement and the circulation of the bass, and I
know that this is so. Then they sigh, and envy affectedly
the happy fate of those actors who had to recite the operas
written by an Alessandro Scarlatti, a Buononcini, or a Gasparini, [A] and other famous men.

But to convince our actors of their affected error, and
make them recognize and say that the fault for the bad recitation is usually ours; it is enough to throw before their eyes
the operas written by Frederic Handel, Porpora, Leonardo Vinci,
Leonardo Leo, Francesco Feo, and Pergolesi, and make them observe and then say whether they still find in these recitatives the supposed interruptions and overturned order of the
music. [B] Let them take in hand those of Baldassare Galuppi,
Christoph Gluck, Niccolo Jomelli, Pasquale Cafaro, and that
master of masters, Giovanni Hasse; I cannot leave out without
great remorse two most worthy masters in this Imperial Court,
which I have venerated, and do now venerate as a duty and for
the chains of friendship. Floriano Gasmann, lately defunct,
who beside his praiseworthy service given in his teaching-
school, has left us his excellent theatrical works. And
Giuseppe Bonno, [C] successor to the latter; everywhere hailed
in fame and name, so known to the musical republic, that it is
only to avoid offending the delicate virtue of their modesty,
that I do not report the universal acclaim which the world
paid them; and this does not mention many others who actually
wrote with much honor. I conclude that no one can with justice envy those days in preference to ours, and can certainly
find the music of all these inferior, and the recitatives no

less well-expressed than those of Scarlatti, Buononcini, and Gasparini. [D]

Thus it is most certain that the decadence of the comic should not be imputed to the *Maestri di Cappella*, but surely to the actors alone. It is they who ruin and ill-use the recitatives, because they do not take the time to learn the rules of perfect declamation.

I do not have the boldness to enumerate the defects of actors, which Pierfrancesco Tosi so well enumerated in his treatise at page 43, so I repeat exactly his words.

He said, "Their defects and insufferable defects are without number, who make recitatives heard without knowing with what they have been entrusted. . .Some sing the recitative in the scene as though in church or in the chamber: there is a perpetual cantilena, which kills: here is one too involved, who howls: here is one who speaks in secret, and is confused: here one who forces the last syllable, another who makes it silent: here one who sings disgusted, another distracted: here one who does not understand, another who does not make it understood: here one implores, here one disdains: here one who is silly, another voracious: here one sings between his teeth, and here one affected: here one who does not pronounce, and here one who is inexpressive: here one laughs, and one cries: here one speaks, one whistles: here one who is strident, another who shouts, and another out of tune; and with these errors which depart from naturalness, the greatest is to not think of the obligation for correction."

I do not know, to speak truthfully, how to understand why the actors, no less than the actresses, hold as vile and not worth care that part of music which belongs to the comic; when they from their own experience and the experience of others, see that well-declaimed recitatives receive no less than well-done arias, the same applause, rewards and honors equal to those that the excellence of singing produces. Let Niccola Grimaldi, called the Cavalier Niccolino, be testimony to this; this virtuoso possessed the comic with such perfection that this alone, had he been poor in other talents and not furnished with a beautiful voice, would have been able to acquire for him the singular merit which he held in the profession. [D]

Why does Marianna Benti Bulgarelli, called la Romanina, remain so celebrated, if not because she was a great actress, and had exquisite comedy to such degree that the immortal Abbate Metastasio wrote for her that great opera, <u>Didone</u>. Or one can cite as comics a Cortona, a Baron Ballerini, a Paita, a Tesi, a Monticelli, and so many others who would enlarge this article if one wished to enumerate them all.

I must confess that a good treatment of recitative will please and entice the listener as much as singing can please

and entice him. We have evident proof of this in the case
narrated by Signor Tartini when he speaks of simple recitative.
   "In the fourteenth year of the present century, " he says,
"in the drama which was being given at Ancona, there was a
line of recitative at the beginning of the third act which
was not accompanied by other instruments but the bass alone,
which gave we professors, as much as the listeners, such a
commotion in the soul that we looked into each other's faces
for the evident change of color which we had all felt. The
effect was not sad (I remember it very well, for the words
were disdainful) but of a certain severity and cold blooded-
ness, which in fact stirred the soul. The drama was given
thirty times, and each time the same effect was universally
felt: the palpable sigh of which was the all-pervading
silence with which the whole audience prepared to enjoy the
effect."
   Another proof of this is that provided for many years
by Gaetano Casali, known under the surname Cavadenti. He
found himself in Venice at the head of a company of comics;
and because the repetition of the comedies did not bring in
enough return, he hoped to increase it through the represen-
tation of the operas of Metastasio. He distributed the parts,
and made the actors learn them, waiting for a favorable occasion to produce them in public. Unexpectedly the first performance of _Artaserse_ in the theater of Saint John Crystothe-
mis was not successful. The shrewd Casali exhibited his own
company the following night at the Cartellone, in the same
Artaserse. The people came in a mob, led as much by the
curiosity of such an unusual thing, which was outside their
experience. But they remained and were overcome, and all
Venice was convinced, because these actors had characterized
so well with their gestures, and well-spoken recitatives, the
personages which they represented, that they won universal
applause to such a degree that they were obliged to repeat
the same opera many times. Casali was so encouraged by the
happy acceptance of his first opera that he continued for many
years to repeat it, which was always sustained with the
strength of perfect comedy alone, and which brought to him
such honor, and profit that he wrote a letter, filled with
gratitude, to the author, recognizing him as the joint cause
of his good fortune.
   Let us here note for our common enrichment, the admirable
effects of well-understood comedy. Works full of seriousness,
written in a style apposite to accompaniment by instruments;
operas whose principal allure should only be singing: and
yet without instruments, and without singing, comedy alone
has been able to render them so delightful as to satisfy every
theatrical type.

71

The *opere buffe*, and the *balli*, which once were written only for intermezzi in serious operas, how could these have arrived together at being able to sustain themselves and be made into principal spectacles instead of accessories, if not through the medium of comedy? The comedians, the *buffi*, with their actions, the ballerinas with their pantomimes, are today the only ones which treat and express good comedy, and are in consequence the only ones who receive the greatest effects of applause and esteem.

I hope that I have succintly and sufficiently proved here that, in order to be a perfect actor, it is not enough to sing well, but to know how to recite well, and to act. It remains only for me to express my sentiment on what should constitute recitative and action.

I say in advance that there are two kinds of recitative; one is called simple, the other instrumental. We call that one simple which is accompanied only by the bass. This dialogue was invented [F] in order not to let the dialogue languish between the arias, duets, terzetts, and choruses which occur in a drama. This recitative, when written by an understanding master, is most natural, because the simple notes which compose it are not only situated on the natural notes of each voice, but are so designed and reappear in such manner as to perfectly imitate a natural discourse, so that each period can be distinguished, and one can mark the question marks, exclamation points, and closes. All of this is expressed in the cantilena, which varies with the movement and diversity of the tones, which change as the sentiments of the words differ, and according to the various emotions which one wishes to a arouse in the souls of the audience.

The other recitative is called instrumental because it requires the accompaniment of the orchestra. Its cantilena is not at all different from that of the simple. The system of the one and the other is always the same; in the instrumental the accompaniment of the orchestra is added, so that it can fill the scene when the actor is constrained to remain mute: and thus it follows throughout, even though the actor speaks, to give greater impact and embellishment to what he says. It is the custom, in order not to interrupt the sentiment and the strength of the expression, to oblige the voice and the orchestra to perform in strict time. This type of recitative was invented for no other reason than to give prominence and to distinguish from all others the principal and interesting scenes, which should terminate with an agitated aria, either of fury or of tenderness. Such recitatives, when well written and well executed, always arouse universal satisfaction, and often are the sole sustenance of a whole opera.

Now the cantilena of the one and the other of these recitatives, however intoned, should always be loosened in such a
manner that it resembles a perfect and simple spoken declamation. Thus it would be a defect if the actor, instead of
speaking the recitative with a free voice, should wish to sing
it tying the voice continuously, and not thinking of ever distinguishing the periods and the diverse sense of the words by
holding back, reinforcing, detaching and sweetening the voice,
as a gifted man will do when he speaks or reads. And here I
lay down another proposition, which I tell you, that all the
merit of recitative consists in knowing well how to place the
appoggiatura, or the accent of the music, as it is commonly
called; this precious accent which is all the pleasing quality
of a beautiful cantilena, consists in a note a tone above that
which is written, and this should only be used on those singular occasions when every syllable making up a word is written
with notes of the same pitch. Here for greater clarity, is
an example.

onde mai tu vedesti

In the preceeding article I have already said what study
the scholar should follow to know how necessary are changes in
the voice; so there is no need for me to repeat it here; I will
tell you only that I counsel undertaking this study in tempo,
that it be done under the direction of a good master, that he
may point out the true road by which profit is won.
I know that among our professors the opinion was at one
time prevalent that the recitatives for the chamber should be
spoken differently from those for the theater, as well as those
for the concert hall or the church. As much as I have reflected on this, I have found no certain reason why there should be
this difference. I think that the recitatives for the church,
the chamber, the theater, ought all to be given in the same
manner, I mean to say, in a natural and clear voice, which
gives the just and complete strength to every word; which distinguishes the commas and the periods; in a manner which ena
enables the listener to understand the sense of the poetry. I
conclude, then, that if there is any difference among these
recitatives given above, it is a difference relative to their
location; this can consist only in the quantity of voice which
the singer, understanding his own strength, ought always to

adapt to the place in which he sings.

But above all; even if the recitative be given with the necessary changes of voice, pauses and periods, it will always be languid and flaccid if it is not accompanied by a suitable action. This it is which gives the strength, the expression, and the vivacity to discourse. Gesture is the thing which marvelously expresses the character of that personage which one wishes to represent. The action, finally, is that which forms a true actor; hence, according to Tullius himself, all the greatness and beauty of the actor, consist in the action: *actio, actio, actio.*

But this is not a pure gift of nature; this is deceit; one can learn with art, and with study. I grant that some may bring from nature, better than some others, a certain good disposition for execution: but the sole disposition for learning a thing is not that it be already learned, but it seems that the more one polishes and perfects with art and with study, the more one loses by relying on nature, and finally becomes rough. They say, it is true, that the action should be natural, and not studied: but this does not signify that one should not study the true manner of acting, but rather that one should not render the action affected, but rather adapted and uniform to the words which one speaks, and to the character which one represents: and this good adaptation and unification is exactly that which they call naturalness, which ought precisely to be learned through study. The good which nature can bring to an actor, is restricted solely to a beautiful personal structure, and even more some elegance in the movement of the arms.

It is true that the study of action does not have sure and precise rules, from which a studious person can learn what precise attitude he should strike on this or that occasion: but there are generalizations which are quite sufficient to form a good actor. The particular rules which one should learn for gesture in this and that case, are all practical, and should be given by mature judgement or learned by attentively observing how good actors act in these cases. These generalizations are theoretical, and can either be learned from a master, or from books.

One of these which is most basic is that of entering the theater with grace, and knowing how to cross the stage with naturalness. All this cannot be learned better than in a dancing school. This teaches to move the feet with grace, to manage the arms, to carry the head, and to move the whole body with elegance. The schools of fencing and horseback riding will also be helpful; especially in cases where the actor must do one or the other of these actions: above all else these render the body robust, agile and loose.

74

To know how to easily and obediently change the face, as it is commonly called, "work with the mask," is also a most necessary thing for the actor. This knowledge of changing the face, showing now ferocity, now sweetness, then tenderness, affection, ire, disgust, according to the affects and impressions which should move, or be received, is in fact the most beautiful part of the action which the actor can use. Everything rests on this change succeeding naturally, and at the right time: thus it is a great defect of some actors, who come into the theater and narrate the disgrace or fortune of a companion, remaining indifferent and in a single humor all the time while the narration lasts, and only at the end of all of this in a moment they give signs of admiration, pleasure, or sadness. These signs, although given with naturalness, ought to manifest themselves little by little, beginning at the moment in the narrative when one can understand something of the whole fact, and growing in extent, as would naturally grow sadness, or anxiety, whichever the discourse should arouse. For this it is necessary that the actor be always attentive and collected, whether he speaks or is spoken to. When he speaks and is distracted, it is very easy for him not only to lose the action, but to go out of the true cantilena; errors which not only offend the ears of the listeners, but can very easily disconcert him and put his companion in greatest danger of failure, when he should be able to depend upon him. If an actor does not pay attention to the speaker, he cannot take part in the by-play, nor explain the internal commotion which this discourse should arouse in him. With all of this one sees far too often actors who, instead of listening to what they are saying and what is said to them, divert themselves either with admiring the scenery, or looking into the boxes, or saluting their friends, all things which are prejudicial not only to the part they represent, but also to the wisdom of a wise singer, and to duty.

In order that the action be perfect, it is also necessary that the actor have accurately by memory all the words and music of his part. If he goes into the scene without knowing them perfectly, basing all his hopes for success on the help of the prompter, and the motives from the orchestra, it is impossible that he will be able to accompany that which he says with any sort of suitable action, since, in this case he must reflect upon the words and music, and cannot at the same time pay attention to and reflect on the action; and being totally occupied with what he ought to say at this point, he cannot prepare what he should do after.

Finally, so that the action be well adapted to the words and person, the actor ought to understand to the bottom everything that he says, and should understand the very particular

75

character of the personage that he represents, otherwise he may make errors which will be embarrassing.

I do not thus think it useless to repeat to the studious youth my counsel and my urgings not to neglect this very necessary study of action. This science is certainly more difficult than one can imagine, but yet we have sure ways and sure means for learning its true rules, and to act with valor. The general rules can be given by the master; the particular ones are learned by practice, by observing the worthiest actors, and by the instruction of a director consulted for precise cases in which particular actions or gestures occur. All the polished cities do not lack for, indeed abound in, these directors, especially in Italy, where cavaliers, literati and civil employees recite dramas for their own pleasure. There are often great comedians among them, and they frequently will volunteer to instruct one if he asks. We have as examples: Marchese Teodoli in Rome: the Marchese di Liveri, and the advocate Giuseppe Santoro in Naples, and many, many others have had the most perfect students, and our own celebrated Abate Metastasio, in our own days in Vienna, when he was still able in the art, demonstrated this clearly with Signora Teresa de Reutter and Angelo Maria Monticelli, who learned so well, and followed his instructions. I finish: if an actor is lacking in action, he is to blame, and cannot excuse himself by saying that he did not have means whereby he could have learned gesticulation.

ARTICLE XV: *OF THE GOOD ORDER, REGULATION AND GRADATIONS, WHICH A STUDIOUS YOUTH SHOULD SHOW IN LEARNING THE ART OF SINGING.*

I had the strongest and most vivid desire to close this small treatise of mine on the art of singing with a collection of select solfeggios from the greatest and worthiest professors, for the pleasure and browsing of youth, that they might reflect and observe what are solfeggios, how they may be useful, and profitable. But reflecting on how many excellent masters there are who teach everywhere, and of what excellent monuments have been left in every style, and especially of the whole study of solfeggio, by the worthy ancients, I put aside my thought as being superfluous and unnecessary; and truly, what could I add to the riches left to us, and of which our profession has fallen heir to in the way of good solfeggios without number, by Leonardo Leo, Niccolo Porpora, and the living Giovanni Hasse, and by many others, from which the masters can draw when they wish to exercise their students; they know that in every cantilena of these solfeggios one finds the highest taste and method of singing, and varied styles in which everyone can exercise, as he thinks fit for himself. Thus the scholar acquires the advantage of accustoming his ear to a cantilena with a magisterial bass, which accompanies and gives help, delight and prominence to the voice; this cannot happen when the cantilena of the bass resembles that of the *colascione*. I know that some will oppose me, saying that these solfeggios "are in antique taste, and passed out of style: because today they sing in another taste." I answer that they deceive themselves; no, such things do not suffer change, because this quality of solfeggio is still useful to the profession, not only because it was written by such worthy masters, but because it was conceived in that time when the manner of singing with perfect taste, with rule, and with precision, reigned; it is so true that with these solfeggios, and with aid of art and the advice of good masters they form those worthy virtuosi and great ladies, of whom I spoke at length in my second article.

I was the student of Leonardo Leo in Naples for two years; and I was then of only fourteen years of age. This great man was accustomed to write every three days a new solfeggio for each of his scholars, but with reflection to adapt it to the strengths and abilities of each. Among my colleagues there were some of greater age than my own, and consequently more formed and more robust of chest. So the diligent and loving master wrote for these, things of greater style for sustaining, and style for agility of voice: I was desirous of emulating my companions without ever reflecting, and one morning when the master presented me with a new solfeggio, I observed that it did not extend beyond the usual system, and taking courage, I said: "Signor, I believe I can sing the solfeggios of my other colleagues, although they are of greater age than I, and to execute them equally as well;" the great master, who had weighed my strengths with the shrewdness of his understand ing, and having penetrated further than I was able, or could; and wishing to correct me to my profit and cut off the head of my capricious presumption; suavely granted my wish.

I began the solfeggio earnestly, and everything went well at first; but, what is this? I became like a baby who under- takes a course of action without measuring his strength, there by loses his breath, falling to earth with a heavy thud. The other things which were more difficult, as much to sustain as to graduate, I knew in that moment to be beyond my ability to execute, because art and strength had abandoned me: then the master with a smiling face turned to me: "I have admired," he said, "your desire, I praise it, but I cannot follow it, be- cause it would upset the order of your studies, and would be your downfall; continue to study with method and patience and in time you will join your companions, and equal them with great glory."

A good document for the studious no less than the masters I document this because I hope that the masters who write for their scholars will learn from it to graduate the solfeggios to the age of their scholars proportionately; and that the wise scholars will elect in the same way the solfeggios adapted to them and their own levels.

Thus can each voice be set upon the road of progress which will most securely lead it to a happy result.

When a small tree is young, it is easy to bend it, and every hand twists it; but if it is pruned it becomes hardened and finally robust and no longer bends, but breaks.

If the masters of music do not complete and perfect this first study at an age suitable to each one of their scholars, they cannot be sure of proceeding to the next study, for they may not find nature so malleable, so disposed to it, and obe- diant.

When the scholar has completed this first study, he should pass to the study of recitative to accustom him not only to place the syllables of the words under each note, but also to render his intonation secure and to put him in possession of free and true cantilena in his spoken recitative. I counsel the masters not to use a recitative of the theater, unless it is written with reflection.

Thus there should be among his collection of solfeggios, those of the cantatas of Alessandro Scarlatti, of the Cavalier

d'Astorga, Buononcini, Gasparini, and Niccolo Porpora, who
has twelve in print, which are truly worthy of such a great
master. As was said in the preceding article, recitative has
its own cantilena, which should not suffer change, lest it
suffer in naturalness of declamation. The masters listed above
have written their recitatives with such excellence, that one
cannot propose a more useful exercise for the young than this,
because they are written scientifically; if the scholar perfect himself with this study, he may be able to appear in the
theater, however young he is, perfect in the declamatory style,
and if he has made profitable use of his time, it can be said
that he recites well.
    The study of madrigals is also quite necessary for the
youth of our times, for such an exercise solidifies intonation,
accustoms the chest to effort, and refines the ear so that it
does not vacillate from the tempo.
    The study of duets is also necessary to accustom the ear
to rule intonation with perfection, and to possess oneself of
expression, and finally to render one practiced in graduating
the voice, so that it is perfectly united to that of his col-
league. Of these madrigals and duets written by worthy masters, solely to the end of producing this good effect, there
is an endless number, known to the whole profession. The only
difficulty is that they should be esteemed by the masters of
our day; and so it is to be hoped that they be permitted and
exercised upon with the just rules. When the schools follow a
good system they do not disturb the order of the study, because
methodically every voice ought to pass gradually through every
rule of the art, and from this it will arise that every voice
will be heard to perfect itself securely in every style of
singing. The most virtuous Padre Master Martini has lately
sent to the printer a collection of duets dedicated to Her Royal
Highness, the Widowed Electress of Saxony, which, as much for
the expression, the grace, the nobility and perfect song, as
for the difficulty encountered in them, difficulties necessary
to render scholars shrewd enough not to misstep, are by common
opinion written by that excellent master himself. If the masters, who are no less than directors of this art, do not lead
their disciples by the right and progressive rules, and do not
give them the just amount of time which is necessary to perfect them with study and time; the success of a good scholar
will be imperfect and unfortunate. They should always have
before their eyes the customs of our predecessors in the art,
and follow their guidance faithfully.
    Domenico Egizio exercised the art of singing to perfection,
and was also a worthy preceptor. Among his famous scholars one
can count Giovacchino Conti, known as Gizziello. One cannot
express the loving attention of the master in instructing him,

nor the faithful execution of the scholar in obeying his master; the one and the other decided not to part until they had arrived at the ultimate perfection. An accident separated them, and a sovereign command from the Imperial Court in Vienna disrupted their mutual agreement. But what is this? The youthful Gizziello, although far from his master, did not fail to put into practice all the advice he had acquired, and to pursue his studies along the lines laid out by his master. He went to England for several years, and there perfected his style, which is indeed a rare one. The high name he had gained notwithstanding, he returned to Italy not quite content with himself, and went to stay in Bologna under the direction of the great Bernacchi. A fact which should be a rule and an embarrassment to many who presume so much for themselves.

The amiable Giuseppe Appiani, called Appianino, practiced the same thing, travelling to Bologna to place himself under the same Bernacchi. This study of these two professors took place at the same time that they were already recognized and acclaimed among the foremost singers. I do not wish that some spirited youths should presume together to abandon the direction of their masters believing themselves gifted with the same talent of the above-named masters! One should guard oneself from falling into this error, for the gifts of Gizziello and Giuseppe Appiani were not only sublime, and rare in regard to singing; but they united in themselves such excellences of custom that they could be distinguished in the midst of all the others in this time of great renown and glory of the profession.

Here I have grief in making known to you one of my doubts Studious youths, I doubt that there is among you the stimulus to perfect yourselves in singing, nor the wish to join to that talent which God has given you, a certain discretion, a certain restraint, a sure humility, which are sure signs of the virtuoso.

I observe that women, because of the charm of their sex, however young they are and not being expert in the art, yet, when applauded, charmed by their prosperity, abandon study as useless; and for this reason they remain imperfect. Young men for the same reason neglect to prosecute their studies, because the master, avid for reward, set them forth first in the theaters, and the applause which they receive deceives the master and the scholar. If the first would reflect upon his interest he would not have himself heard by the public until he was perfect; and if the second believes that these applauses come from the public because of his present merit rather than to give him courage for further hope that he will improve his talents with greater study, for in fact, what merit can a youth of sixteen or seventeen years have? He can only demonstrate a good

quality of voice and a good disposition; but the rest he must
acquire by toil and fatigue; and in fact how many youths of
good expectations remain like ships stranded on dry land near
the port. Do you know from what this disorder arises? Behold.
Here is a youth gifted with a gracious voice, a charming portamento, a well-made person, of amiable and pleasing features.
These extrinsic qualities will produce applause for him, and
love; he becomes vain, and puffed up with wind, and does not
study further; if this one, and others like him, returning to
their native lands from performing elsewhere, should follow
their studies with more zeal, with application, and let themselves be taught, they could hope to arrive at perfection in
the art: but oh my! the predominant ambition, which is like
a secret among us of which each wishes to believe the opposite,
is that all of these will finish as dust: some will remain
among the first rank; some become insufferable, and some completely incapable.

Indefatiguable study, true and sincere docility, love for
great effort, true humility and civilized behavior are the
qualities, the necessary virtues, which make a great professor, and make him distinguished in our profession, by all the
world. [A]

The End. [B]

APPENDICES

VARIATIONS AND REVISIONS IN THE EDITION OF 1777

The edition of 1777 was called forth by two events: The publication in 1775 of *Regole armoniche*, by Vincenzo Manfredini, and the encouragement of Padre Giambattista Martini and others. No doubt the laudatory letters Mancini mentions in the Preface to the new edition, given below, pleased him and made him aware of the value of his work. Padre Martini was especially impressed with the book, and a letter, apparently in Martini's hand, has come down to us; I append a translation at the end of this section of revisions.

Manfredini's book contained a rather vicious attack on Mancini, and the reaction to this can readily be seen in the sections which Mancini amplified for explanatory purposes. He defends his position on intonation, for instance, with great force, and points out the most serious argument against Manfredini, that he was a theorist rather than a practical teacher. The tempering of scales was coming into common use at this time, and Mancini's position prevailed.

Martini's suggestions resulted in amplification of the mention of Italian singers of rank and worth in the second edition, giving us an interesting view of the contemporary evaluation of singers. Farinelli retains the first place in Mancini's estimate.

Whatever other motives Mancini had for bringing out this second edition, we must be grateful; several areas were enlarged and made more explicit. The only loss in this series of changes is that what had been a teacher's personal expression of methodology, took on the character of a generally applicable textbook, styled after Pierfrancesco Tosi's justly renowned *Observations*. Padre Martini's letter encouraged this broadening as it compared the various treatises on singing which he felt to be of value. History has confirmed Martini's judgement.

The mechanical indication of revisions and alterations is indicated by the insertion in the text of the edition of 1774, of letters in brackets; by referring to the appropriate Article in this Appendix, the reader can interpolate changes. I have not burdened the reader with every word which Mancini changed, unless it had some definite bearing on the technical matter under discussion. The present edition is designed for practical use, and Mancini re-wrote some sections in more fluent and updated Italian, without basically changing the sense of the text. However, transpositions of large sections are noted, for these were made for purposes of emphasis and continuity.

There were only three musical examples in the edition of 1774; these were enlarged to thirty-one in the second edition, and placed all together in a table at the end of the book. I have followed this same procedure, tipping in the text those examples which were in the original edition, and including the rest at the end of this Appendix. Example 1 does not exist in the edition of 1777. The original clefs have been retained in re-copying these examples, for the sake of historical curiosity. They can easily be transcribed for modern use by remembering that the C clef always indicates the line on which Middle C falls. The whole of the plate bearing example thirteen was re-printed in the edition of 1777, the only change being in example thirteen; the occurrence in the second plate has been indicated as example thirteen-A in our transcription.

The Dedication is different, a Preface has been added, and some changes made in each Article. The original edition bore the imprint, *Vienna, nella Stamperia di Ghelen, 1774;* the edition of 1777, *In Milano MDCCLXXVII, Appresso Giuseppe Galeazzi, Regio Stampatore. Con Approvazione.*

The title of the original edition was *Pensieri, e Riflessioni Pratiche sopra il Canto Figurato.* The words 'Pensieri, e' were dropped in the 1777 edition, which is called, erroneously, *Terza edizione.* This may be a mistake on the part of the printer, but more probably refers to the French edition of 1776, translated by Defougiers, and published as *L'art du chant figure.*

DEDICATION

TO HER ROYAL HIGHNESS, THE MOST SERENE MARIA ELISABETTA, ARCH-
DUCHESS OF AUSTRIA, ROYAL PRINCESS OF HUNGARY, AND OF BOHEMIA,
etc., etc.

GIAMBATTISTA MANCINI.

Numbered among the many virtues which luminously adorn
the spirit of Your Royal Highness, is the science of Music,
and the Art of Singing, which through diligence, study and
happy success you have cultivated. Thus it is that I offer you this series of my thoughts, in which I recount all
that which experience and meditation have taught me is most
pleasant in my profession. This work came to light first
with your exalted name in the front, a major excellence which
one cannot improve, and cannot extol enough; but bringing it
forth again, it seemed to me susceptible of enlargement and
correction

Deign, Most Serene PRINCESS, to accept happily the reforms, and to honor them with your benign glances. Permit
me to once more present, and consacrate to you this most
humble public tribute of respect, gratitude and veneration.

PREFACE

Occasionally accident, but often utility, has made a
place for the arts, and they have been allowed to fade with
the fading of their utility. They have been ruined by the
ruin of centuries; some have not surpassed the mediocrity in
which they were born, as one observes principally in China.
Many were in diverse times more or less cultivated, in
the measure that the interests of nations or individuals
rendered them advantageous and opportune; a few of them
were gradually refined to perfection. The major part of
the arts, which had their cradle in climates sufficiently
happy and favorable to their cultivation and possession
without interruption, have been transported from Africa to
Europe, from Egypt to Greece; from Athens to Rome; but the
desolating anger of many northern peoples, who inundated,

devastated, divided and destroyed the Roman Empire, lower-
ed the veil on the Empire of Constantine, interred the arts
in barbarism, along with their cultivation; thus the precious furnishings of many original productions of industry,
and of the talents of our greatest men, were annihilated.

The fine arts were recalled to new brilliance after
this dark epoch and the oblivion of many centuries; it was
necessary to gather the few remains of them, left behind
by the general calamity, for imitation.   Imitation of
the most beautiful originals and the best exemplars teaches
not a little, and one may thus acquire cultivation in the
arts;(however, a common error is to frequently confuse
perfection in a work with small realization of its defects; from this is born that servile imitation which in
some ways weakens and insults the perfectionability of
humanity, as Marmontel wisely observes in his article,
Criticism.)   Thus it follows that painters, wishing to
test their pupils, give them some pictures by Raphael
to copy.   But not all the arts have perfect models,
on which the cultivators can form themselves.   Do not
doubt that the Art of Figured Singing is one of those
whose existence depends more (although often less fruit-
ful and more tiresome) on instruction by precepts, than
on examples.   The precepts and theories should be in
every age the elements and the fountainheads of every
science and every art; but since man comes from the hands
of nature wholly ignorant, he can possess nothing unless
it comes from his observations and the deductions of experience, and is thus fixed.   Thus experience herself is
the wisest mistress in the arts; in Music principally,
those who have had the most experience should possess the
most understanding.   I do not wish to flatter myself at
this point; but considering the advantage to the profession, I wish to present those enlightenments which the
exercise of my profession in many years has brought; I
published in Vienna in 1774 some few of my Thoughts and
Reflections on Vocal Music, for the use of those who teach
no less than those who study.   My efforts were accepted
not only in Italy and Germany, but also in France, where
they were translated into that language in the year 1776
by Signor Defaugiers; and a little later in the month of
March they were honorably mentioned by Signor the Abbate
Rozier in his *Literary News* at page 261; but since I felt
that I had omitted some reflections in the first edition,
and they would be useful, I began for my own entertainment
to write them down, and add them to these many others.   The
insistence of friends, the authority of professors, who all
encouraged me to reprint my slight production, gave me the

courage to undertake to purify it, and with great attention
to enrich it, as I have done. Have no fear, I could produce the most gracious letters I received on this point,
from Padre Martini, from Giovanni Hasse, called *Il Sassone*,
from Gaetano Latilla, from Niccolo Piccini, from Giovanni
Amadeo Naumann, and other most worthy professors of our
art, sent to persuade me; but they are too favorably written in regard to me, and too full of unmerited eulogy. Filled with such ponderous authority, and hopeful of contri-
buting, however slightly, to the betterment of all, I have
not quailed at putting to the torture all my abilities, however small, to reshape, amplify and perfect, as much as possible, this small treatise of mine. I hope that the professors will look kindly on what I have said for the advantage of youth. I hope that the youth will profit from this
occupation of mine; here they will find instruction and food
for thought, and they will be enriched by the nobility of the
art; and excited to place their feet firmly on the road to
understanding of perfection and honor.

ARTICLE I

[A] Among the many remedies against boredom which humanity has invented, needful of an occupation; among all the objects which occupy the imagination and the sentiment, have no
doubt that Music is among the richest and most perfect, able
to make one forget the ills of life when it uplifts him; it
can improve an already fine and delicate sentiment, provide a
more exquisite pleasure, and reveal a better existence, when
it entices and renews us.
[B] The origin of music is extremely old, since the vocal
(which is more despotic, and quite dominates the affections
and the human heart, since it is most close to the original,
that is, it follows nature closely) is surely coeval with the
world.
[C] The following is added: . . .the savages themselves,
who live among the woods like wild beasts, have their songs,
some of which have been recorded by the celebrated Rousseau
in the last table of his *Dictionary of Music*.
[D] Add: and by consequence of having been cultivated
by every kind of person, if I should add to the given generalizations luminous examples, very many would underscore this
history, so sacred and profane, in proof of my assumption.
[E] The most holy Archbishop and protector of Milan, St.
Ambrose, applied himself to this art in such a manner that,

88

especially in the sacred hymns to God, designed to elevate
the people, he is considered the inventor, and from his name
it took the name of Ambrosian Chant. Saint Gregory reformed
the ecclesiastic chant, and introduced especially the In-
troits, and this method of singing took the name Gregorian
Chant.

[F] Not only the heroes of antiquity cultivated music,
but even the legislators and the highest philosophers believed they could not ignore it without blame.

[G] In a word, all the writings of antiquity contest,
and give full faith (Footnote: *Luciani Gymnast. Plutar. de
Music.*) to the concept that music in those times passed for
an art necessary to all persons of good breeding; to such a
level that those who did not understand it were regarded as
persons without education, in the same way that we regard
those who do not know how to read. On this proposition one
can read the dissertation perfected last year at the Royal
Academy of Mantua, and published in their acts.

[H] St. Augustine, who wrote seven books on the subject,
reasoned profusely on music; and in fact, in book four at
chapter four, on the Trinity, he teaches that all men by in-
stinct understand the suavity and strength of musical harmony; even uncouth men, who have no skill in music, understand clearly the effects. I produce these assertions for
those who are not content with the proofs supplied them by
daily experience, or who have not reflected on this point as
much as they should.

And in fact, if everything that is today written and
seen regarding the miraculous effects of music were out into
practice, there would be no more cause to encourage persons
of every rank to cultivate it. By an occult divine strength
it seizes the heart, moves it, ravishes it and changes it by
its talent. Now it perturbs, now quickens, now fills it with
love, now with pride, now arouses a smile, and now a tear,
all through the secret work of harmony, and especially
through the virtue of song.

[I] Music has often been adopted for the relief of the
ill; and not a few doctors have used it, as is testified to
by the Acts of the Academy of Science of Paris for the years
1707 and 1708. Similar facts are reported by Georg Franck
von Franckenau in *Satirae medicae XX*, Leipzig, pub. by Maur.
Georg Weidmann, 1722 in 12, at page 464,[1] where a medical
dissertation *de Musica* is found. Macrobius, *Lib. 2. in somn.
Scip. c.3,*[2] says that Music also cures bodily disease.
Martianus Capella [3] maintains that the ancients cured
fevers with song; and by means of the same, wounds were heal-
ed; (perhaps the soul, exhilirated and uplifted by Music
flowed through the body and excited restitution of strength

in its parts) and the Asclepiadae(4) returned hearing to the
deaf through the sweetness of sound; Thales of Crete drove
off pestilence and other infirmities. Nicodemus Frischlin
in *Oratio pro Musica*, 1574, p. 204 (5) speaking of Clinia
Pithagoras, says that he had recourse to the lyre as the most
secure medicine, to cure his rage whenever he felt himself
being transported. That music cures the pestilence and other
ills, Galen asserts in *De sanit. tuend Lib. I.C.XI.*(6)

I shall add here another fact known to all whom it
pleases to keep informed of the anecdotes of the lives of
famous musicians who flourished not long before our own times.

A person of Wealth sent two assasins to Rome to avenge
himself upon the person of Alessandro Stradella, famous musician and composer, who was to be killed. When they arrived
they inquired where they might find the unfortunate man they
had been sent to murder; hearing that he was then at St. John
Lateran, to sing an oratorio of his own composition, they went
immediately to that Basilica, in order that they might recognize him and follow him until they had been able to accomplish
their avaricious cruelty. Stradella sang with his habitual
sweetness and suaveness, so that the assassins, penetrated,
moved and conquered by the melody of his song, not only put
away all thought of gold and blood; but called aside by those
treasures which in certain happy moments open virtue in every
man, repented of having assented to this inhuman design; filled with remorse for having violated the precisious days of
such a rare artist, they proposed to respect him as sacro-
sanct, and in fact to serve him. To this end, when the func-
tion was over, they opened their souls to him, as to why they
had come to Rome, not only to reveal the hatred of him who
had sent them, but also so that he could escape and avoid per-
secution and revenge.

---

(1) *Franckenau, Georg Franck von (Giorgius Francus de), c.1676
1749, Danish physician. The correct title as given by
Forkel: Dissertatio de Musica, medico necessaria, habit.
1672 Ejusdem Dissert. medic XX, Leipzig 1722.8. p. 464-
499.*

(2) *Macrobius (Ambrosius Aurelius Theodosius) fl. c. 422,
Roman commentator. Forkel gives the title as: Commen-
tarium in Somnium Scipionis a Cicerone descriptum, Liber
II.*

(3) *Capella, Martianus Mineus Felix, fl.c. 450-500. Forkel's
title: De nuptiis Philologiae er Mercurii, libri duo.
Parm., 1494.*

(4) *The Asclepiadae were a sect of physicians on the Greek
island of Kos, of whom Hippocrates was the best-known.*

(5) *Frischlin (Frischlinus), Nicodemus 1547-90, Prof at*

Tübingen. Forkel gives the title: De Encomico Musicae,
Oratio. No date.
(6) *Galen, c. 130-c.200, Greek physician and writer.*

ARTICLE II

[A] Although the rules and the fundamental laws of music
are common, and followed by necessity everywhere, the variety
of their application, as much to instrumental as to vocal
music, renders the execution enough different to affect more
or less the pleasure which is produced thereby. Since the
scope of my work is to treat vocal music, or singing, I shall
explain here the different methods, or we should say systems,
being followed.

[B] I will not speak here of the singing school of other
nations, but rather intend to speak only on the Italian, because I know it, and professing it, have room to make the
reflections set forth in this treatise.

[C] Footnote: The industry used by Fedi in Rome is
singular, and his school was the most celebrated in Italy in
the last century. Angelino Bontempi of Perugia refers to the
worthy singers who often led their scholars to a passageway
where they found a famous echo outside the Gate of St. Paul,
and here had them sing in loud voices. The echo which is
nothing but the repetition of the voice of him who sings, exposed to the singer the defects of his singing; and thus the
scholars, convinced of the evidence of their defects, found
it easier to correct them. These excellent masters were joined to Bernardo Pasquini, organist, and harpsichordist, and
with Arcangelo Corelli, most gifted composer and violinist.
They found themselves often united, and this was useful for
communicating the beauties of their profession, and from their
common light all the many illustrious students who came forth
in great numbers, profited.

[D] Ed. Note: Mancini has added the first names Giuseppe
Ferdinando Brivio, Francesco Peli, Francesco Redi, Giuseppe
Amadori, Niccolo Porpora, Leonardo Leo, Francesco Feo; and
the name of Domenico Egizio in Naples.

[E] Many are the scholars sent forth from these schools,
made famous as much for the art which they professed as for
the number of new students they formed, transmitting thus
with an uninterrupted succession to this one and that one
the beauties of the art itself, and the most natural and
easy modes of overcoming the obstacles in executing it.

91

[F] There flourished at the beginning of this century Giovanni Paita, the splendor of Liguria, born in Genoa, so famous for his singing, as well as for his pantomime that he was held to have few equals; and Francesca Boschi, of Bologna, for her rare merit and celebrity called the Solomn of music by the Venetians

[G] Footnote: He was added to the celebrated Philharmonic Accademy of Bologna in the order of composers in the year 1690, and was the Principal in 1708 and 1710.

[H] This is changed to read: It is enough that I say that he was universally admired in Italy, England, Germany, and especially in the Court of Bavaria, where he served for many years in company with Bartolino of Faenza.

[I] This fact alone is a self-evident lesson of the advantage which a scholar reaps from the assistance and advice of a good master, and the fruits which he can expect from his own application, to the point of being able to render natural defects insensible, and to master the organs of the voice through a long and determined habitual study, so much so that a bad voice becomes not only mediocre, but may even become good.

Mancini adds a footnote here: He was added to the list of the Philharmonic Accademy in the capacity of composer in 1722, having learned the art of counterpoint in Monaco in Bavaria from the celebrated Dr. Giuseppe Antonio Bernabei, and in Bologna from Giovanni Antonio Riccieri. Bernacchi was Principal of the Academy in the two years 1748 and 1749, and obtained from Pope Benedict XIV, of holy memory, a Brief in favor of the Academy, which destined the masters to be vigilant that ecclesiastical music be decent and proper to the Majesty of God, and to approve those who wished to serve as composers of sacred music in the City and Diocese of Bologna.

[J] Among the number of his best scholars, most of them now carried off by death, the tenor Carlo Carlani, of Bologna, is worthy of memory.

Mancini added footnotes on Amadori: Singer of the Royal Chapel in Naples; and Guarducci; *Virtuoso di camera* of the Grand Duke of Tuscany.

[K] Footnote: The terms here and other places used to distinguish the qualities of singing and the excellences of the artist, having been generally received in all the schools of music, and having a determined significance, do not require to be further explained.

[L] This voice did not lack for sufficient agility, for a solidly perfect trill and mordent, which all united gave him ability to execute every characterized style. He possessed the musical accent to the highest degree; and since profound wisdom was united in him, the whole of his singing

was in an accomplished and well-bred style, and he fully
earned the name of most wise artist.

[M] Also from Bologna came Annibale Pio Fabbri, called
Balino, scholar of the above-mentioned Pistocchi. He was one
of the most excellent tenors of his time, and was heard in
all the leading theaters of Italy, and beyond, decorated by
various Princes, especially by His Christian Majesty the Emperor Charles VI, who honored him by making him the God father
of one of his daughters. He was added to the Philharmonic
Accademy as composer in 1719, and was Principal of the Academy
in 1725, 1729, 1743, 1747 and 1750. Then he was called to
Lisbon to be the singer in the Royal Chapel, and there he
died on 12 August 1760.

[N] This example is enough to make it clear that a good
and worthy master cannot hold to one method for teaching his
pupils; to form perfect singers, he should know profoundly
the diverse manners that he may take up and judiciously apply
in practical cases, following need. He who possesses this
talent, is held, and always will be held, in high esteem by
the cognoscenti of the arts. The singer should guard against
the too common defect of wishing servilely to imitate whatever he sees and hears executed by others in the profession,
because it will often be to his prejudice, and instead of
bettering himself, he will lose those graces acquired by having followed his natural disposition and measured his own
strength carefully.

I do not intend by this to exclude some imitation,
because from this comes one of the perfections of music,
from which one draws that fine discernment and that just mod-
ification, which the talents of each person render necessary.
A good imitation of that which the best original singers do,
should be admired, because it is a difficult thing to carry
off.

[O] This reads: In the same time that these last named
musicians were the delight of the greatest and most renowned
theaters in Europe, there were not a few gifted women of equal
excellence who were beginning to carve out careers in music.

[P] This is not the sole example of the value of recognizing one's own strengths, and examining the natural disposition, which each one must find through study and the corresponding mode of living. It is certain that la Tesi, by
her voice alone, and her singing alone, however perfect this
was, would never have acquired the celebrity which was hers,
but for her sublime manner of declamation. Covered with
honors, la Tesi died in Vienna 9 May 1775.

[Q] Footnote: Giovanni Hasse moved to Naples in 1722
to follow and perfect himself in the art of counterpoint
under the direction of the celebrated Alessandro Scarlatti.

It is not right for me here to exalt with my words the profit
he gained therefrom, because while quite young, in a brief
time he made himself known, distinguished and admired throughout Europe. With his marvelous productions this distinguished
artist, after having written with reiterated approval various
opera for the best and diverse theaters in Italy, took up the
service of the Royal and Electoral Court of Saxony, where for
many years he has written the most beautiful music for Church,
and operas for the theater, where they must have always new
and refined compositions to satisfy the exacting tastes of
the Sovereign. For some time the professors of the art have
wished that this great man should give to the Public by means
of printing, if not all, at least in part, his so lauded works
to serve as models and instruction for studious youths. He
is, however, excessively modest, and to this day has not ac-
ceded to this insistence, so that the desires of the cultivators of music remain deluded to this day. While he took
up the service, as I have said, of the Elector, he has not
failed in diverse years to travel into Italy, where he wrote
operas, always well received and applauded. His great fame
caused him to be called to Paris under the rule of Louis XV,
King of France, and also to Berlin by the reigning Friederich
II, King of Prussia, where he had equal success, and reaped
universal admiration. Also in the Imperial Court he has received many distinctions and benefices; and lately the uncon-
querable Empress Maria Theresa, gloriously reigning, has been
served by this master on the luminous occasions of the various
weddings in the Imperial family.

The epoch of this great man has been fairly short, but
yet we see that in every time and every place he has been
appreciated as he deserved, and now he lives placidly in
Venice, full of glory, and for his excellences called by the
professors, Father of Music.

[R] Before being married she was called to London, where
she was accepted so gratefully that this country was enchant-
ed by her extraordinary merit, and wished to retain her for
many years. When she was called back to Italy, she contracted
her marriage with that illustrious Master, and united with
him, accepted Royal service in Saxony, and since she made
trips always with her husband, dividing the honors with him
everywhere, and she is now his companion in Venice in a tranquil life and honored repose.

[S] Mancini amplifies this passage: . . . passes and passages executed in varied styles, now legato, now vibrant with
trills and mordents; now staccato, now held back, now filled
with redoubled volatinas; now with a few leaps tied from the
low to the high; and finally by perfect execution she gave
perfect attention to everything she undertook; all was done

94

with surprising finish.

[T] Beside those singers already named here, many other musicians and singing women attracted the admiration of Italy, as much for the harmony of their voices as for the happy method managing them, and they have won the title of meriting entrance into the history of the music of our times.

[U] Footnote: Singer of the Royal Chapel of Naples.

[V] Mancini adds: was called to Spain, to Paris, to London, Vienna in Austria, and finally to Lisbon. . .

[W] Footnote: Gizziello was Neapolitan; Fontana born in Turin, scholar of Antonio Pasi; Regginelli, born in Naples; Amorevoli was in the service of the Electoral Court of Saxony.

And Mancini adds: I should say only that all of these, beside having been gifted with beautiful voices, had such a good understanding of the method of singing to which their natures inclined them, that they applied themselves with purpose, and were well directed by their masters, obtained well-earned constant public applause and were everywhere well received.

[X] Footnote: One counts from the year 1740.

[Y] This lady had a pure and sonorous voice: it was according to the helps of art, and became perfect in varied styles. She was brought forth in several seasons in the principal theaters of Italy, where she obtained the most desirable success. Finally, moving to Madrid, she sang for several years with the highest distinction in that Royal Theater.

[Z] Teresa de Reuther, born in Vienna, and *Virtuosa da camera* in the Imperial Court, became celebrated as a singer in several styles, in agility, in sostenuto, and in the expressive style, added to the vivacity and talent of a good actress.

[AA] Caterina Visconti, called la Viscontina, born in Milan, was a scholar of Ferdinando Brivio. This lady became an extraordinary singer, gifted with a voice of good body, made light, proportionate, sweet, and of rich extent. She handled perfectly every style; but she distinguished herself above all others in agility, executed without trouble, wherever she encountered it, however difficult. She was besides a most capable actress, for which she was acclaimed everywhere that she was heard.

[BB] Giovanna Astrua, born in Turin, was perfected in singing in Milan under this same Ferdinando Brivio. This lady, because gifted with a very agile voice, applied herself to that style so assiduously that she rendered her voice apt to surpass every difficulty: she sang no less well in sustained style, which she embellished and revitalized with all those graces which sensitivity alone produces, joined to wisdom and delicacy of good taste. She was admired for

95

several years in the first theaters of Italy, and finally took Royal service at Berlin, where she passed many years with the highest satisfaction to the Royal Court.

[CC] Regina Valentini, called la Mingotti, born in Naples, and her parents were German nationals: in her youth she was taken back to the city of Gratz and sent to the Monastery of the Ursalines, where she received her education. Her great application was for singing, and she believed so strongly that she could become one day a good singer, that even while young she was taken into the service of the Royal Court in Saxony, run by the celebrated Niccolo Porpora, who was living there on a pension, and spent his time as he would, in a school of singing. In the progress of time she returned to Italy, and became admired in the principal theaters, not only as a virtuoso singer, but also for her quality as a good actress. Her singing, to be frank, was not so extraordinary for agility of voice, because she did not execute anything but what she needed for ornamenting a few characteristic cantilenas; but she had a certain grace in presentation, in pronouncing, in sustaining, in coloring the diverse sentiments, all accompanied with the most natural noble gestures. In Naples especially she aroused all to transports, and left a universal desire for her presence when she was called to Spain, and went.

Caterina Gabrielli, of Rome, having studied music in her one country and in Naples, appeared first at one of the theaters in Venice. The superiority of her talent was immediately recotnized, and then she was invited to Vienna, where she stayed for some time, always applauded. Then she sang at the major theaters of Italy, and at Petersburg, and at London, with equal success.

[DD] This has been changed to read: It would take too long if I spoke of other singers of the first rank to the same extent that I have so far; there are many of superior merit, flourishing very much, and many of them are to be heard now in the theaters, and occupy positions destined for the most virtuosic professors: it is enough that I list their names, which are all known throughout the world of music.

There are Domenico Anibali (Born in Macerata, in service in the Electoral Court of Saxony), Giovanni Manzuoli (Born in Florence, virtuoso da camera of the Grand Duke of Tuscany), Filippo Elisi (Born in Fossombrone), Antonio Hubert, called Porporino (Born in Verona, in the service of the Royal Court in Berlin), Giuseppe Santarelli (Born in Forli, singer in the Papal Chapel), Cavaliere Gaetano Guadagni (Born in Lodi, Cavaliere of San Marco, Philharmonic Academy, who lives today in Padua, and is associated with the Chapel of St. Anthony), Ferdinando Mazzanti (Born in Tuscany), Giuseppe Aprile

(Neapolitan, and a supernumerary in the Royal Chapel), Pasquale Potenza (Neapolitan, singer in the Chapel of San Marco), Giuseppe Millico (Neapolitan), Carlo Concialini (In Royal service in the Court of Berlin), Venanzio Rauzzini (Born in Rome), Ferdinando Tenducci (Born in Tuscany), Giambattista Vasquez (Born in Domaso, in the region of the Lake of Como, in the service of the Court at Lisbon), Antonio Goti (Born in Tuscany, virtuoso da camera to the Grand Duke of Tuscany), Giuseppe Cicognani (Born in Cesena), Gasparo Pacchierotti (Born in Fabriano, supernumerary of the Royal Chapel of Naples), Salvator Consorti (Born in Ascoli, my native land, singer in the Royal Chapel of Naples), Giovanni Rubinelli (Born in Brescia), and some others.

Among women have been distinguished Rosa Tartaglini, wife of the great tenor Tibaldi, of Bologna, died 17 November 1775, Lucrezia Agujari (Born in Ferrara), Mattei, Anna de Amicis (Born in Naples), Elisabetta Teyber (Born in Vienna, Austria), and Antonia Girelli Aguillar.

My readers will think it marvelous that I can advance the opinion, after such a great enumeration of worthy singers, among whom are not only Italians, but also some from across the mountains, that our music has become decadent, and that good schools and good singers are lacking.

I must confess, that if such an opinion be false in regard to the schools, yet is it quite true in respect to the singers, among whom no one has been seen to arise to fill with honor the void left by the old artists. It is beyond doubt that there are plenty of youths gifted with talent, and the qualities necessary for attaining excellence.

The origin of the evil, to my way of thinking, lies with the vile interests which seem to dominate the great majority of the masters, who are not content to apply the good rules of the art, and the precepts transmitted to them, and fail to give the necessary attention to the diverse talents of their scholars, not thinking of starting them on a career unless they can see them immediately placed on the stage and bringing in a profit, which they stipulate to be taken from the profits of a student, who are sent forth immature, and often win flighty applause, abandon their studies, and fail utterly to advance in the secrets and refinements of their art. How then should one hope to see numerous troops of good musicians issue from schools run in this disorder, where the students are encouraged to avaricious cupidity by the masters, who give a few years of free lessons, in order to regain through usury long and enduring profit, caring more for the number than the quality of their students? Is it possible that a youth, after flying over the rules of music, which for another require to be learned by long habitual study, and made capable of half-singing a few arias, and a motet or two, should become a good singer? After this, is it not certain that the best talents will be lost, for lack of correction of defects at birth, which become incorrigible with time? Beside all these inconveniences which are presented easily to the eyes of those who know the profession, these is also the problem that the youths, abandoned to themselves in this important hour, and then put among persons who are not the most well-behaved, cause themselves prejudice to their health, and ruin forever the voice, the chest, and by bad example lose the vision of the best moral behavior.

Another very grave inconvenience is, that today many set themselves up as singing-master, without ever having learned practically the rules of the art, and without knowing in the least how to lead their pupils, and teach them perfect intonation and exactness of tempo. These persons believe that it is enough to know how to play the violin, or play the harpsichord a little, in order to be singing-masters, and offer their slight work at little cost compared to that which a good and patient master must charge for his devoted diligence, they can find persons whom they can seduce with the apparent advantage of a secure bargain, and who entrust themselves to their direction. These inexpert masters think they have done everything when their scholars execute this or that passage, although imperfectly, and a few shrieks of the voice which offend the ear. Such is the instruction which is given by many teachers in our time, and such is their knowledge.

It is a real profanation of the art, when a simple and bad player of accompaniments, or string player, arrogates to himself the quality of a master of singing, without knowing the first elements. They make their students shout with the fullness of their breath, ruining beautiful voices, not knowing the means for producing and extending them, and one hears inequality of registers, discords, voices in the throat, in the nose, covered, because these masters pretend that the scholar should execute with the voice what they execute with their own instruments, whether they be harpsichord, violin or cello.

And how, from all of this, can excellent singers come forth? Let the reader judge how desirable it would be for this kind of school to cease to exist, and how propitious for the young, if none should be admitted to the ranks of masters, unless they know how and wish to put into practice the true method of instructing, disinterestedly and paternally.

[EE] The conservatories of Naples are three, those of St. Mary of Loreto, that of St. Onofrio, and the other the Pieta de' Turchini, founded in 1583, restored in 1592.

In the first we can actually say that the first master

is Signor Pietro Gallo, second Signor Fedele Fenaroli, and
third Signor Saverio Valente. In the second, Signor Carlo
Lotumacci, Signor Giacomo Insanguine, called Monopoli. In
the third, Signor Lorenzo Fago, Signor Pasquale Cafaro, master of the Royal Chapel and the Court, and in his place in
the conservatory, Signor Niccola Sala.

Here the young are taught not only art gratuitously, but
also religion and good conduct. Establishments so useful to
the country and easy on the families have given Italy the
major portion of her celebrated professors, in whom she can
glory, as I shall add in Article XIV.

The conservatories named still perfect many in singing,
whose fame and worth are known, and of which Italy can give
proof in every time. A major advantage to the young is that
those who have not enough talent to succeed in secular life,
and brighten all the theaters, are led into ecclesiastical
life, and they procure from the governors of the conservatories sufficient position and upkeep in the diverse cathe-
drals. It is desirable that in the future many of those noble
souls will be born who benefit humanity, by propagating and
establishing additional institutions as advantageous and opportune for the perfection of music, good conduct and religion like those of whom Naples and Venice alone can brag.

[FF] In fact in painting there are the masterworks of
the immortal Raphael, Correggio, Titian, Leonardo da Vinci,
Domenichino, Guido Reni, and other equally gifted painters;
in sculpture the most noble remains of the Greeks, like the
Apollo Belvedere, Niobe, the Gladiator, the Knife-grinder,
the Antinous, the Laocoon, and many other divine works. In
architecture the beautiful pieces preserved in the passage
of centuries are the ancient temples, edifices, circuses,
etc.; and the original works of Vignola, Pallades, Scamozzi,
etc.; finally in the art of composing music the productions
of Alessandro Scarlatti, Bononcini, Vinci, Pergolesi, Sassone,
Jommelli, and of many other most worthy men, are all helpful
to lead one on the way by perfect models.

The precepts thus deduced from the contemplation of all
that has been done in the fine arts mentioned above, forms
a new systematic guide for advancing and making use of strong
study in order to become excellent.

ARTICLE III

[A] The first three paragraphs have been changed to read:
The corruption of taste has become so effeminate in Italy,
having taken it as necessary to please a preference for a kind

of voice, which mostly extends itself to the highest notes, that it is not hopeful that this taste can be easily changed, for men are thereby sacrificed to diversion and other delights. It would be desirable if only the number of these were not so great, and that the parents were more often moved by sentiments of piety and by moral principles, and would not destine almost any son to singing without regard. Since this is a most important point, I do not wish to avoid saying what I should at this point, from pure Christian charity.

Oh, one should not expose his children, or before he exposes them and dedicates them to singing, it should be the duty of parents to assure themselves through rigorous examination whether they are furnished by nature with all the necessary qualities needed for singing, in order not to put them in peril of being forever unhappy. According to the materials which I propose to discuss, it is enough to say, that one should not proceed with children who are of too tender age, it being still uncertain what disposition they may have for singing, because the organs of the voice lack their consistency until the age of puberty. And if that disposition is lacking, behold how many children would be rendered useless to themselves and to their native land, because placed in the position of not being able to take up any other calling with chance of success.

[B] Beside this general advice, which does not seem to require much examination, because they depend upon the first impression which the subject's appearance makes, there are others much more delicate and difficult, which can only be made by one who understands the method in which the vocal organs work.

[C] Mancini adds: . . .but it is true withal that the voice remains somewhat defective, especially if the operation is not made in time.

[D] Mancini adds: . . .who had already for a long time practiced the profession of singing;

[E] This paragraph is deleted entirely in the edition of 1777.

ARTICLE IV

[A] Title change in edition of 1777; *OF THE VOICE IN GENERAL, THE REGISTER OF THE CHEST, AND THE HEAD OR FALSETTO.*
The following was added: I cannot better begin this article on the voice than by adopting the words of the illustrious Jean Jacques Rousseau in his highly esteemed *Dictionary of Music.* "Voice," he says, "is the sum total, or bringing

together of all the sounds which a man can make singing with
his organs. It is different in different persons, like the
physiognomy."

Since nature rarely is prodigious in making all her gifts
to one person; thus it is rare enough to encounter all the
qualities which form a perfect voice: and thus it is true
that we encounter some strong voices, whose sounds are strong,
impetuous and flowing; one encounters others that have sounds
flexible and sweet; one finds a few that are robust, sonorous,
and of not mediocre extension; one admires some that are beautiful and pleasing, which give out a sound that is full, accomplished, harmonious and pleasing. On the other hand, one
encounters some voices that are hard and heavy, others flexible and light, many of whose sounds, although beautiful, are
inequally distributed, and there are yet again those who make
the same quality of sound in all their ranges; but of these
various defects I shall speak in the seventh article. In
order not to wander aimlessly in long discussions on the qualities of low and high voices, and on their distinctions, deduced from the octaves through which they extend, nor on the
rules, nor the limits which contain the voices of Bass, Tenor,
Contralto and Soprano, I will content myself with speaking
only of the voice as it is commonly considered and distinguished among the practical use of artists.

[B] In the edition of 1777, Mancini has extended this
to one note higher, D-la-sol-re on the fifth line, Soprano
clef.

[C] In the case where the scholar does not have great
strength of chest, he will find it reasonably easy to sing
to C-sol-fa-ut, but will require more force to get the voice
to the limit D-la-sol-re.

[D] Then if the scholars are lacking in strength, it
should not be too difficult for them to reach in the first
register to B-mi, but they will find more difficult the passage to C-sol-fa-ut. Now this greater or lesser difficulty
so sensible in the indicated cases, is easy to distinguish
for whomever pays the least attention, and if he wishes to
deduce surely the change of the voice, when he arrives at the
termination of the first register, entering the second, finds
it naturally weaker.

[E] This is changed to read: Experience demonstrates
all that I have so far said. It will convince anyone who
takes the trouble to observe attentively, that the chest voice
is not equally true and strong in everyone, but that some will
have robust or weak organs of the chest, and thus will have
more or less strong voices.

[F] The great art of the singer is to render imperceptible

to the listener or the watcher, the greater or lesser degree of difficulty with which he brings forth the voices of the two different registers of chest and head. This can be obtained only through endless refinement: but it is not easy to master this in a simple and natural method. One must use study, effort and industry to correct the defects provided by the greater or lesser strength of the organs, and one reaps a management and economy which render the voice equally sonorous and pleasing, which few scholars reach, and of which few masters understand the practical rules, or how to execute them. Far from accusing the voice in the terms adopted in the profession, of being inimical chords; every singer who finds himself in these circumstances should accuse himself, or bewail his own master, who has not known how to put him on the right road. Since this is a most important matter, I have thought to treat it separately, as I shall do further on, indicating the methods by which one can render every defect insensible which arises in the singer from the causes mentioned above.

I am content here to add, that there are not many roads for arriving at this intention: and that it is useless to believe that one can attain this end by any other means, besides this single one, of which I have the wisdom of persons of diverse abilities, and following them, one will never force nature.

[G] This paragraph does not appear in the edition of 1777.

ARTICLE V

[A] What I have already said, will convince sufficiently those who wish to destine themselves to the profession of singing, that they ought to have regard for many things, and that intent observation alone can guide them in this. I am especially firm in speaking on the causes which determine a good voice, in order to give a norm for recognizing such a one, and judging what it may become.

[B] Grandual says (1) on this proposition: "I found myself present one day at a kind of small concert of two or three persons; a concert which had not been premeditated, and which had no other origin than this occasion. A young lady, who knew music mediocrely, but who lacked any ear whatsoever, sang through a whole scene a complete semitone above the accompaniment (a habitual vice with the young, to sharp, contrary to older singers, who flat without realizing it). The father who had no more ear than his daughter, but had an unchangeable good opinion of his discernment, did not cease to

102

be ecstatic, throughout her noisy dissonance, and then I
understood, that one lacks for little if less comes to him.
Nothing more remained to reduce this concert to perfection
but the introduction of a *tromba marina,* as Signor N.N. would
have it."

(1) *Forkel gives this name as Grandvall; the title of the work
is: Essai sur le bon gout en Musique. A Paris, par Prault,
1732 in 12, p. 8.*

[C] This judgment is not difficult to make; but one
wants experience, and there is need not to hurry, or fail to
make opportune reflections to convince oneself, and be sure
of the results. One should make the youth sing more than
once at the harpsichord on various days; observing that now
the sky is serene, now cloudy, that the air is sometimes pla-
cid, and in others the wind is agitated and jerky, and that
he is sometimes hungry, sometimes with a full belly. If then,
despite these precautions, he invariably sings out of tune,
and after having been often advised and corrected, when he
takes up singing again he continues to sing out of tune, then
one should frankly judge and assert that the defect is natural,
or comes from a bad organization of the ear.

Since this is, as I have said, irremediable, and since
every study would be in vain, and every effort which one might
try to correct it in the young, the honest master can do nothing in this case, except to advise his parents so that he
will not be made to lose uselessly the best time in that
school, but can rather be destined to other science or art
right away.

[D] Signor Manfredini, in a work entitled *Regole armoniche,* published in Venice in 1775, at page 11, undertakes to dispute my proposition, and asserts frankly that
these instruments are adapted to accompanying a voice.

I value greatly the worth of this brilliant professor,
but I had hoped that his assertions would be made in regard
to beginning scholars, to whom I have made mine. In fact,
anyone who knows music, knows the oldest of the old rules,
which is that for accompanying a professor of singing, one
should adopt on the harpsichord a few fingers only, and
should not wish to add ornaments capriciously, but rather make
use of the most solid and simple accompaniment, so that the
singer is not disturbed in any way. Yet it is another thing
when one speaks of accompanying a young student who is not
yet sure in his intonation (and this is the case of which I
speak in my book). These instruments of slight strength are
of little use. I call upon the experience of a hundred who
often have had nothing but the help of their strongest harpsichords to rule and sustain the intonation of their scholars,

and are obliged to play with all the fingers, and add to all
this their own voices, and I am persuaded that if there were
pedals on the harpsichord, as there are on the organ, they
would have used these, too, to sustain through any means at
hand the intonation of their scholars.

If Signor Manfredini were as experienced in the practical teaching of singing as he is worthy in harpsichord playing and the art of composition, as he demonstrates in the best
thing contained in his operas, he would certainly have passed
over the censuring of my proposition, which lies outside his
own observation, which comes to me from the most express in-
terrogation of the celebrated masters in the art, and stands
recognized as self-evident, and a true and constant practice.
Yet he says that it is against reason to teach with the harpsichord half out of tune, which I admit: but this is a failure of the masters, if they do not insure that their instruments are well-tuned. He also says that the true method of
rendering a musician capable of singing by himself rapidly,
and without bad intonation, is to make him understand perfectly the distance which lies between one tone and another,
whatever the degree of leap. No one could doubt this, but
the difficulty consists in pointing out the way, which will
teach this most easily, and render the scholar sure in its
execution. The method proposed to us by the aforementioned
Manfredini, as the most apt to strengthen the scholar in intonation, is not now used by any master; it would be practi-
cable only with professors, and never with beginners; so the
wise masters, in order to secure the intonation of their
scholars, retain the praiseworthy and useful customs of sug-
gesting that they not sing beyond a certain tempo. This
author has maintained from his earliest youth, that one should
hope to fix the intonation with the sole assistance of one
voice, accompanying the bass. It seems difficult to believe,
that a professor of such worth as is ascribed to Signor Manfredini, ignores how many years a musician must study and
exert himself, before he can sing alone; or rather one should
say when he arrives at this point he may be called a professor
I have here spoken only to scholars, and not professors. I
must add here some things which the perspicacious sagacity of
Manfredini has not arrived at recalling; if the master be of
advanced age, or has a bad ear, or through some other defect,
does not intone exactly the bass note, the scholar must remain
embarrassed, if he has not absorbed the rules and fruits of
good instruction. He says finally that it is a different thing
singing the notes as they stand written, and as they are sound
ed by the harpsichord, with grace and expression. Let everyone notice that in the second case the aid of the voice of the
master is indispensible for success; but this does not lower

104

the usefulness of the master in the first case for sustaining a fluctuating intonation, and the help of an instrument
which accompanies loudly enough to be heard by the singer,
and does not contradict the habit of knowing exactly the note
sounded, and the ability to intone it correctly at every
occurrence by himself. Above all at the beginning let us remember to instruct the scholars in the fundamentals of the
profession, then in the outlines of graces and customs; otherwise the singers and the pretentious virtuosi will ignore
music forever, and become one of those vocalists who is incapable of singing a few notes which he has not already seen.

[E] It was established by the Greeks, taught by observation, that the human voice naturally extends itself through
two octaves to the number of fifteen diatonic notes (Fig. 1)
(1). In our times this has been refined greatly, and since
compelling nature, the voice of the singer is extended to a
greater number of notes, because that singer is esteemed as
more excellent who has the greater number and extension of
notes. Even better is the excellence of him whose notes are
equal in worth, and perfectly in tune.

---

(1) *Figure 1 is missing in the edition of 1777, and no corresponding figure is found in the edition of 1774. The figure
inserted by Buzzi in the edition of 1912, must be of his
invention.*

[F] In proof of this one can observe that the masters
of counterpoint have taught their students that the leaps of
the perfect fourth, diminished fifth, the seventh, major,
minor or diminished, ought more often in composing to be used
in descending than ascending.

The reason for this is that they are more natural, and
the lower notes are more easily given than the higher notes,
which can often be given only with forcing and discomfort.
Thus the greatest care is necessary on the part of the scholar, to render him able to treat this portion of the voice
with the required sweetness and proportion, so that he forms
the entire register perfectly.

[G] And here I should advise, that when the human voice
is accompanied by instruments which differ in tuning and
temperament, the singer will often find himself embarrassed
and undecided as to which instrument he ought to follow, and
listen to.

Everyone knows that the organ and the harpsichord are
stable instruments, and have the intervals (except for the
octave) tempered, that is, somewhat diminished or increased
in regard to justness and precision. Bowed instruments, the
violins, violas, violoncellos and violone, are in themselves

both stable and instable; stable because the strings remain
steadily tuned in fifths or fourths. They remain moveable,
however, because they are touched by the fingers, and successively one can bring forth various pitches with the bow. Win
instruments are by nature stable, but as the wind is more or
less forcibly blown, often the wind can change their pitches.
To this defect the most excellent professors have found a
remedy in the exact moderation of the breath.

From all this one derives the fact that the singer, inclined by nature to just and precise intonation of the intervals, finds himself not a little embarrassed to know which
of the diverse temperaments he should follow. He should perhaps force himself to follow the tuning and temperament of
the organ and harpsichord, because these, although tempered,
and thereby imperfect, have been retained as the bass and
standard for all, including the voice because of their con-
struction and the difficulty of reducing their tuning to that
of any other instruments. Lacking a harpsichord or organ,
the singer should always adjust himself to whatever instrumen
which has been adopted by the others as the basis for their
tuning, this being usually the violin, which for this reason
is called the first. (1)

It is to be desired that the player of the above-mention
ed instrument which serves as the standard, has a most perfec
ear, and that he use great diligence and exactness in tuning,
so that the temperament, inevitable as it may be, remains only slightly noticeable, and the singer can then lean on the
tuning of the whole.

------

(1) *In the supposition made here, which probably will be quit
rare (since singers rarely submit to singing with the accompaniment of instruments among whose numbers neither organ or
harpsichord is found) it becomes necessary that they procure
the tuning of the instruments through the use of a tuning-
fork. The reason for this being that the professors of the
violin, persuaded that their instruments sound better when
tuned higher, always follow this principle when tuning them,
and the singer cannot easily follow them.*

[H] The theory of music teaches us that the distance between the D-la-sol-re sharp and the E-fa-la on organs and
harpsichords is about two commas, and if the singer wishes
to be an exact observer of the fundamental canons of intonation, he should not fail to temper both, increasing the sharp
a little, and in the same way lowering the flat, and thus in
this place making two pitches, since one alone could not render their differentiation sensible.

Here is the cause for the intervals altered by a sharp

seeming to be stimulating and rough, and the intervals flatted being similarly softer and more languid.

[I] This great man was convinced that it was necessary to place ones attention on the essentials, and not on accesory parts, so he thought of a way to explain the road to his disciples, and abandoned the composite and most difficult old notation, making up one which was equally good from the foundation up, so simple and easy that it tyrannized his beginners less, and in brief was such that without sacrifice anyone with a bent for the art could gain immediate and useful instruction.

Others should do the same in imitation of this master I have mentioned, and seek new methods of notation which would be even easier and less laborious for the scholar.

[J] Footnote: The author of this new method of solfeggio is the very noble Cavalier Signor Marchese Fulvio Ghigi Zondadari of Siena, who published the following book: *Riflessioni fatte da Euchero Pastore Arcade sopra alla maggior facilita, che trovasi nell'apprendere il Canto con l'uso di un solfeggio di dodici monosillibi.* (Reflections made by Euchero, Arcadian Shepherd, on the greater ease which he found in learning singing through the use of twelve monosyllables.) Venice, printed by Carlo Pecora, 1746, in 4. This most worthy musician and Cavalier, having made a collection of writers on music which is one of the most unusual there is, applied himself to seeking out the easy method for solfeggio, and was induced to publish it under the name of Arcadian, not letting his modesty and moderation suffer from using his own name. Since he passed to a better life several years ago, and since a well-founded notice of him has come to me, I think it best to tell the public.

[K] The essential point which must not be lost sight of in this notation or in any other, is that the masters be the most rigid observers so that every note is perfectly in tune.

The previously mentioned author of the *Regole armoniche* has his own opinion in this regard as well, and at page 5 and 6 treats himself to making critical observations on the method of teaching notation given here. On what basis, or with what reason, one can judge from what follows.

Speaking of natural sounds, he gives the rule *octavus itaque sonus similis est primo.* This is very old in the art, and known even to beginners. He goes on to say: "The other five sounds, which on the harpsichord are found interposed among those of the octave, not entering into the quality of tone, nevertheless do not occupy a different place on the lines or spaces, and a simple sign such as the sharp or flat is enough to make them recognizable. Therefore they do not need a different name, and should that be necessary, one would not be enough for each key, but one should rather want two, that is, one for the ut-sharp, and one for the re-flat, since these are two tones totally different, although it is not so on the harpsichord,. Even more, if the semitones are to be called by the names, pa, bo, tu, etc., how shall we name the si-sharp and the mi-sharp, which are sounds no less important in harmony than the others?

He pretends that they should be called by the name of the sound whose position they take. For example, the mi-sharp should be called fa, because on the harpsichord that is how it happens; but at this point the gravest error occurs. It is true that on the harpsichord the mi-sharp becomes a fa, because such an instrument does not possess a separate key to express this sound; but it is also true that the mi-sharp is not truly the same sound as fa; and in fact in keys where the mi-sharp has a place, the fa does not, and vice versa, in those where the fa has a place, one cannot have the mi-sharp. The same is true of sounds that are not natural, and specially of the fa double-sharp, which should not be called sol, as Signor Mancini says at page 60; but since it is a true fa in the harmony, and occupies that place in the staff, one can only call it fa, and in sounding it raise it a half step or a whole step, according to the accidental which marks it. It seems to me therefore that the system given is not completely necessary, nor all good, since the famous Guido D'Arezzo invented the six syllables ut, re, mi, fa, sol, la. The syllable ut was later changed to do, since the u is a vowel ill-suited to singing, and the same applies to the syllables pa, tu, etc., which are just a little adapted to forming a good voice."

Here ends the author cited. The defects which he mentions are so well known that it seems useless to discuss them even with this certain air of novelty.

If he wishes to merit attention, let him propose some new idea for a harpsichord or organ or other instrument which would not be defective. Not having done this, nor having any hope of seeing it done by others, he can only join with all the other professors who suffer in peace the instruments name which in spite of their defects, serve as a standard and rule for tuning so many other instruments, and for the direction of many voices.

The disgrace of the century obliges professors to content themselves with the good and renounce the best, because as yet no instrument has been found where one can indicate with half-split keys all the sharps and flats. Since the difficulty of playing so many keys discourages the men of the profession from reforming the harpsichord, it is best left to those who wish to make abstract speculations, which are of little or no use in practice.

Perhaps one should mention that, since the actual notational systems are made up for the harpsichord and organ,
others would have to be devised if new and more perfect
machines were invented, capable of giving to each key the
true name and distinguishing it from the others, as seems to
be the scope of what Signor Manfredini has said on this
point.

But in order to render more distant the criticisms of
the above-mentioned author, and make their insufficiencies
even better known, regarding the sharp and the flat, let us
reflect a little more on what he has said. He asserts that
these "have neither line nor space, and do not therefore enter into the quality of tones." Had he taken into account
the precepts of the art, he would never have pronounced a
sentence so dry and absolute.

He could have recalled that the keys of music, when they
are occupied with sharps and flats, are called "Transposed
keys." He could have reflected that this distribution is not
arbitrary, but rather necessary, otherwise the two semitones
of the octave would be subjected to meeting together outside
the prescribed intervals.

The professors and master composers of music do not ignore this established order of sharps and flats, and they do
not require further explanation. He who wishes only to sing,
and not enter into the arcane and into the art of composition, there is no necessity for knowing the theory, the rules
for fixing transpositions, and the effect this produces. It
is enough for such a one to know the alteration which arises
from the sharp, the diminution which the flat carries with
it, and the effect of the natural. It is enough for him to
know that the one and the other, when placed near the clef,
reappear on the lines and the spaces, called naturals, throughout the entire composition, on all the notes which they desig-
nate, except for the natural, which requires its own changes,
etc.

One calls the sharps and the flats "accidentals" when
they are found occasionally in the course of a cantilena,
designated at the left of the note. This clarification is
common among us, since it is taught among the first rules of
music, and is called the ABC of music.

In order to prove that the sharp can establish a key,
it is enough to consider the case of the key of C-sharp Major,
which carries with it seven sharps in order to render its
movement perfect (Fig. 2). The same follows when the key is
determined by flats, as in D-flat Major, which requires five
flats to fix it well in key (Fig. 3).

If then these signs are necessary in order to establish
a major or minor key, what reason can one give for leaving

them out?

Let us proceed. In order to demonstrate the infallibility and justness of this new notation, and prove it by examples, which do not themselves determine the naming of the notes, and consequently aid the intonation by whatever sound they fall upon, I shall take first the ut-sharp, which one may see in Figure 4.

In order to understand that the same keys serve for the sound of re-flat, look at Figure 5, and one will see that it differs not at all from Figure 4.

Enough has been said regarding the difference between the D-la-sol re-sharp and the E-la-fa. For this reason the reader was warned by me, closing this article in the first edition of my book, censured as it was by the author cited, where I said what I have repeated above. "Everything rests on the masters being rigid observers, so that each note is perfectly in tune."

And who does not feel the sharps to be exciting, and the flats insensibly more moderate? In fact, while the ut-sharp and the re-flat are the same sounds on the harpsichord, they are nevertheless arithmetically different, as experience with the monochord teaches us.

I add to all this, that this arithmetical division, however visible in theory, is almost insensible in practice. And so it is true that the master, if he hears an ut-sharp sounded in tune and then a little later a re-flat, out of tune, has no other recourse to correct the intonation than to suggest it with the harpsichord, with the voice, or with the key alone, if the instrument be well tuned. The thing being so, the sound agrees with the notation, and this unchangeable correspondence is exactly what makes both notation and intonation easy. The cited author cannot be persuaded how to name the si-sharp and the mi-sharp. If he will observe Figure 6, he will see, according to the rule, he will see how the si-sharp is named. If he passes then to examine the key of ut-minor (Figure 7), he will see that this tone corresponds to the same keys as Figure 6.

For the mi-sharp, although it is not the same sound as fa, one should not change the intonation which belongs to it, but rather encourage the scholar to call it fa, because it truly falls upon that sound: see Figure 8.

One may then speak in the same way of fa-double sharp: glance at Figure 9, and you will see that this sound lies on the key for sol; and even though it is so, Signor Manfredini wishes us to call it fa, according to his system, that is; according to our system founded on the instruments which we possess, and on constant observation, one must of necessity call it sol; just as a different name does not produce bad

110

intonation, neither does vocalizing it; thus the scholar can
keep the fa-double sharp perfectly in tune using the name sol.
He believes he can defend his position by saying, ". . .and
in fact in the keys where mi-sharp has a place, one cannot
have fa, and in those where this latter has a place, mi-sharp
cannot enter. The same goes for all the other tones, etc."
But this explanation gives even greater weight to our own notation, for he who knows what accidentals may fall in the keys
of B-fa and F-fa-ut, etc., will know also that no mi-sharp
can occur. From all of this it follows that in the named keys
a fa accompanied by its proper consonances will be to every
eye and ear a genuine and natural fa. If one sings in the
chromatic tone, the mi-sharp will also be called fa, and one
will see that it joins perfectly with its just and respective
accompaniments; and in consequence the notation adapted by
me will produce perfect intonation for the voice.

   If the profession should abolish the syllable ut invented
by Guido D'Arezzo, and establish in its place the do, I will
never say that the change is not for the better, however the
vowel is, of the five vowels, not good for singing, nor for
the voice, as is recognized by experience and unanimously confessed by the professors.

   The new notation, however it may seem in respect to the
five syllables which fall upon the middle keys of the harpsichord, if examined with an impartial eye, will be found not
so different from the old system. Let us see: the syllable
ut was not invented by the author of this notation, named
above; he has adopted it anew, putting back into use this invention of D'Arezzo.

   In order to make an exact comparison of the other five
vowels, which fall upon the middle keys, I shall say that the
pa refers to the syllable fa; bo to do; tu to ut; de to re;
no, once again to do; and si to mi.

   This discovery, if it has not met with the approbation
of Signor Manfredini, nevertheless merits more than a little
notice, and the greatest and most able professors have been
able to lead their scholars easily along the difficult road
of singing, finding that they owe this profound and judicious
Cavalier the highest praise, and recognition rather than cen-
sure. And finally it is without doubt, known to all, that
not every vowel is equally good to render singing sweet. Here
the ability of the masters comes in, for they must know how to
exercise their scholars, vocalising them in the manner which
will best lead them to beauty and perfection in singing.

   I conclude this article, somewhat beyond the intelligence
of beginners, to whom my labors are directed, by saying that
it is not necessary to tie oneself to one notational system
or another. Every master believes his system the best, and

on this understanding I have proposed my own, leaning on
the long experience which I have, and on the equal success
of other celebrated masters, who have found that it served
them fruitfully.

It is not to be hoped that notation is unchangeable,
for the forms of the notes were established in 1350, as they
exist everywhere, received with such ease by all the nations
of Europe.

ARTICLE VI

[A] . . . which, although at first glance do not seem
of great importance, yet form one of the most essential points
for good success.

[B] No one, at least to my knowledge, has treated this
part of the profession as he ought, and I myself did not reach
fixed ideas, except after a series of observations, and after
the experience of many years.

[C] This is a talent which cannot be acquired except after having seen the practice of worthy professors, having followed their footsteps, and with other things, including the
right experience, recognized the most natural and sure road
to guide beginners well. Every time that the master has himself exercised the art of singing himself, there is no doubt
that he is in a position to instruct others.

[D] In fact, it is not enough to know the profession well
enough to sing a few arias in good taste, mixing in ornaments
and graceful passages, in order to expect to be able to teach
with any probability of good results. He should be accustomed
to the method of producing the voice pleasingly, of opening
the mouth, and executing appropriate ornaments and passages,
in the best manner. Without this, only rarely will the master know how to recognize the ways to proceed with differen-
scholars, nor know how to lead each one of them to open his
mouth in the required proportion, nor conduct them insensibly
to the best execution of the passages and ornaments mentioned.

[E] This passage is changed to read: Above all the qualities which are desirable in a master, that which is regarded
as indispensible, is good communication in instructing his
students in the rules of the art, without ever wearying them
too much, something often encountered; and what nature does
not give liberally to many, the rest can hope with study,
patience and time to acquire. Certainly it is desirable for
a scholar to be instructed by a master of such a temperament;
and he is fortunate if he encounters a master who is facile,
loving, patient, untiring, who knows his temperament and the

disposition of his talents.

Since, as I have said above, it is a very important thing for the singer to know how to open his mouth, because upon this depends the clarity of the voice, I shall limit myself to speaking of the defects which can be committed in this part, in order to let you know how they may be remedied.

The first is to bring forth the voice without paying any attention to the opening of the mouth, and opening it badly, that is in such a way that the voice does not come out clear, sonorous and beautiful.

[F] Having advised you that the rules for opening the mouth cannot be general, one cannot establish any universals for all individuals. Anyone can see that nature has not provided an equal opening of the mouth to everyone. One has a very large opening of the mouth, one medium, and another even less: notice that the height and length of the teeth is in some larger and in some smaller. All these differences, and others depending upon the structure of the organs of the voice, oblige the master to observe diligently in which opening of the mouth the voice sounds most clear, purest and of greatest range; from this he can judge how much the mouth should be open.

Further, experience teaches that an opening which is too large or too small, besides looking ugly and deformed, will render the voice ungrateful and disgusting. I am of the opinion that this knowledge, firmly established, and taken as an essential, is one of the most important things for a singer. Without this, and abilities in other parts of the profession not withstanding, one cannot arrive at pleasing, and will remain ridiculous and repulsive.

[G] First, the voice has, so to speak, a certain quality of sepulcre and deadness:

[H] . . . through which the forced air seeks an outlet, not finding freedom anywhere else.

[I] General precepts are almost useless; but practical applications are somewhat efficacious. To indicate precise rules, the master should show the scholar, and make sure that he sees, the true and perfect position of the mouth. He will see how much better this method is than a general statement, with which he disapproves of the opening of the mouth of his scholar.

[J] Footnote: Signor Manfredini does not cease to assail me from every side. He has also attacked me on the vowels, ignoring the fact that I have said it is difficult to pronounce the vowel I when singing, and according to him anyone who sings it ignores the rules of art. Art and the experience of many years during which I have seen and touched with my hand, teaches us that forwarding the mouth too much and

grimacing too much in pronouncing the vowel I in singing together give a dull sound, little pleasing; and on the contrar
a smiling mouth, composed with naturalness, enables one to
obtain that grace and sweetness which are so necessary to the
pronunciation of the I, and so pleasing to the listener; on
the point the masters and the professors of our art can decide whether or not I speak the truth.

[K] And so the master should attentively observe what
position as we have already discussed, gives the scholar the
greatest advantage, and exercise him in that, putting his
natural disposition to profit.

[L] This exercise in singing from memory should be used
only in the daily lesson, designed for the acquisition of the
portamento of the voice, and in solfeggios which should exercise the agility, etc.; the rest of the study should be done
in the usual method, so that the scholar becomes honest and
secure in every musical composition.

If the scholar sings his daily lessons without defect,
in front of his master; so then one may hope that he will do
as well in every other lesson, for a good custom once taken,
cannot be changed, even if he is not seen by the master.

ARTICLE VII

[A] There is no room here to enter into the painful and
tiresome enumeration of the gradations of defect voices. To
make you understand, and to be useful, without diffusing myself too much, I chose three types of voice which are the mos
vulgar and common, and for each I shall propose the corresponding remedy.

[B] In this case it is certain that singing at full voic
and failing to use the art of producing the voice with modera
tion, graduating each note of length with just lightness of
breath, so necessary to set it, he cannot be saved from his
shortcomings; on the contrary if he sings under the direction
of a good master, with moderation and thought, he will erase
with a minimum of effort all his defects, and will be able to
guard against their reappearance.

This so essential method for firming up a voice should
not be overlooked, but should be introduced, so that the scho
lar may become strong in his singing, his scale well in tune,
and his leaps regular, so that he learns to graduate his voic
well according to the precepts of the art.

Here is the system, which is the unique method for
strengthening the voice, exercising it on white notes, given
with justness and taken one after the other with the necessar

radation. The strengthening of the voice should be succes-
ive, and as opportunity presents itself in accord with the
trength of the scholar; and this growth should be pushed for-
ard by the master, without hoping to get to the desired re-
ult too prematurely; but little by little he should lead and
ix the voice in that level which he knows is suitable.

I cannot hesitate to repeat that which I have already
entioned previously, that is that a continual habit of exe-
uting well and following the road laid out by the master as
est for the student, is the sole means by which the rules
iven can be made useful and efficacious. Natural defects,
nd those brought on by bad direction, can only be destroyed
hrough a long series of actions, the object of which tends
o correct the faults of the organs and the musical education.

[C] This is a most prejudicial error both to the beauty
f the voice and to the strength of the chest. Experience
eaches us that rather than force the voice, one should ex-
end and strengthen it without fatigue; that is to say, with
he moderation of the breath make oneself even better heard
y the listeners, without tiring and weakening the chest of
he singer.

This is an art known to few, which should be understood
nd practiced, so that the voice is conserved strong and
leasing even into old age, as is seen in the experience of
elebrated singers of a time not far from our own.

ARTICLE VIII

[A] Art consists in knowing where nature directs us, and
o what we have been destined; understanding at once the gifts
f nature, cultivating them easily, man can perfect himself;
ow sure is harvest for the attentive farmer, who has observ-
d and understood the different seeds, which are fecund in
iverse types of earth.

Thus the master should be advised to not betray the scholars, and the scholars not to distrust the inclinations of
the master in regard to nature, which, when overlooked, makes
every attempt to overcome or correct by the aid of art, futile.

[B] In regard to solfeggios, there are few masters who
give enough diligence and mastery to how they should be composed; one hears once in a while some compositions so barbar-
ous, without naturalness, without sense and good taste, that
instead of teaching, annoy and disgust the nature of the young
singer. Use therefore, every study in composing solfeggios,
that they be natural, grateful and well directed with good
modulation, and when one cannot do this himself he should make

115

use of those written by those learned in the art, because this is a point of great importance, on which depends a special profit of the young singer.

[C] This reads: Practical application will show clearly that the scholar should, according to a precept of the art, give with his voice the first note lightly and little by little, and ought, by another precept, to pass, without taking breath, to take the second with the same gradation, as much to obtain a good effect, as to conserve the breath with that good economy which, in going ahead, will accustom the lungs of the voice to regulate, gradate and take back the breath, and will make him master of taking breath, according to need, with insensible effort and fatigue.

ARTICLE XI

[A] This section which follows has been added to the edition of 1777; it replaces the first paragraph of the edition of 1774:

Nature has in certain cases administered her gifts to man in a manner which is rough, uncultured and imperfect. The genius which creates, the sentiment which examines, the taste which judges, the reflection which corrects and perfects, helped by the subtleties of art, with the exercise of the human faculty can reduce the gifts of nature to their best point, and make them conform to the delights of the intellect and the heart.

In the pleasing variety of forms of the animals we admire the diverse gifts of nature diversely distributed with economy and partiality. The faculty of producing sounds remains untouched by the inhabitants of the water, and in large part remains the province of those who live in the art, the principal element, in which sound is formed (1), and without which all nature would be mute.

Man cannot certainly pretend that the height of the beauties and graces of nature has been reached in him alone; what merit can he have in preference to other animals in their view? Unjustly, truly, he has pretended to equal the birds in singing; although he has been gifted with articulated sounds in plentitude. Yet following his natural impulses and cultivating his own faculties, exercising, perfecting, he arrives at outstripping the best and most perfect models which nature has given at first hand in singing.

The graces and the ornaments by which human singing rescues itself from natural roughness and near-barbarity, and

116

only by acquiring these ornaments, without which it would be empty and tasteless, are: the portamento of the voice, the appoggiatura, the messa di voce, the trill and the mordent.

I have already spoken of the portamento and the appoggiatura in the preceding article; I shall treat of the others in following articles, gradually, beginning by telling here of the messa di voce.

---

(1) *There is no doubt that music, principally vocal, can acquire lustre and growth to the extent that the acoustic is perfected, and light is shed upon the human constitution and organization; in the same way painting has gained much from optics and perspective. We ignore whether the inarticulated sounds of animals can be rendered articulate, or whether many small animals produce any sounds at all; when some ingenious inventor has taught us to arm the ear, not only these, but many other beautiful inventions, both useful and pleasing, can perhaps be acquired, in not diverse guises, as the invention of the magnifying lens has allowed us to know of the existence of many minute and invisible beings which live in parts of other beings.*

[B] Add Figure 12.

[C] This reads: I should say, then, that if one wishes to formulate this without defect, it will be necessary that the scholar not force the breath violently, but produce it quietly; in other words, he should make it with an exact economy, producing it little by little, and this being done, he can with sureness take the first note, beginning very sotto voce, increasing little by little to the loudest degree, then taking it back by the same gradations he used in reinforcing it. In this way he will find out how to sustain it to the end, and avoid that inconvenience which befalls singers who find themselves out of breath, and who produce the breath with impetus from the beginning, making the tone of the voice go sharp, and at the end go flat, making two manners of the whole, and singing discordantly, to the displeasure of the audience.

ARTICLE X

[A] The following long section was added to the edition of 1777:

The most painful and tiresome period for one who applies himself to the study of any art, is that which is devoted to the necessary acquisition of the elements and the principles of the art.

I do not enter into the question of finding out whether
one may treat better, or more advantageously and briefly instruct youth, because I have directed these reflections of
mine to practical application alone, and not to theory. The
cowards say, the labor irritates them, that the elements and
the principles of the art are a useless language, unintelli-
gible and superfluous to the creative genius, which without
them can lift itself upwards and expire the most noble flights
They say that the rules and methods of our best practitioners
are examples of their smallness and pedantry; even so they
cannot deny daily experience. And yet why did Vergil, Tasso,
Metastasio, although gifted with sublime invention, and creative genius, seek out the study of the elements, and follow
the precepts of art in composing? No one can deny that in
every art necessity requires the study of several years on
the first necessary elements, which serve as the base and
sustension of the art itself.

Thus it is that the studious cling to the idea that it
is indispensable to cultivate oneself in our art with scrupulous diligence, so that one can grow in the measure allowed
by the age and the strength of each individual, each type of
voice, and the precepts divided by me in the preceding articles, on whose good use depends the perfection of singing.
It is in these years that the master, reflecting upon the
ability and the progress of his scholars, can study and understand their dispositions to good or bad results, and from
certain predetermined indications can know whether his student will become an extraordinary, good or mediocre singer,
of sublime ingenuity and ability, gifted with expression, or
bereft of every gift of voice to that extent that he will be
called a musician of notes and words, giving all to expressions and gestures, etc.

These signs are more visible in the course of each individual's study for those who take them into consideration,
and in fact those masters whose credit is somewhat equivocal
because they are Ancients, were exact observers in discover-
ing them, and did not allow their students to wander from the
moment they began their studies, so that they were not lost
in the diversity of ornaments which embellish singing.

They passed their years in perfecting their intonation,
in exercising to insure the firm sustension of the voice, to
clarify it, increase its strength, to learn to produce it, and
graduate it, etc.

One single ornament of our own style was given to these
students without delay, that is, the trill. This ornament,
whether a natural disposition was observed or not, was required of every student to be exercised in good time, not to

render him perfect at first; but to facilitate the eventual success and to introduce little by little the motion which is necessary to it. Thus when the student is placed upon the road at the right moment, perfection can often be attained without difficulty and loss of time.

Today this so essential system has been completely reversed, because today's masters are so avid to collect glory and money, sending out their scholars in the weak age of their first years, and to compound their disgrace they require them to sing arias of Caffarelli, Egiziello, Ferdinando Mazzanti, professors all known for their rare merit, acquired through an assiduous study directed by profound wisdom, judgement, art, and the experience of many years.

This newcomer, what effect can he hope to make? I say to him: This will produce the ruin and the waste of the most beautiful voices, which should, according to the rules of art, be gradually mastered, becoming beautiful and good, each in its own style; but when they are entrusted with a burden they cannot sustain, it only follows that when they sing everything is badly executed, with a weak and childish voice, because they lose their strength, which only through time and use and regular exercise can be obtained.

The Public in such cases says frankly: "This voice is bad, it has neither agility, nor strength, and yet wishes to sing agility: this other has no trill, nor a good chest: this other should be bearable, but Good God, he sings in the nose, etc."

These masters, then, whatever the outcome of their students, care little, as long as they rake in the money and accumulate gold. I do not believe that the success of modern students can be better, because they are raised up and praised without the first and true elements of the art, without a graduated method, and they are expected to give ornaments and graces of singing which are both imperfect and counterfeited, among which is the terrible trill indicated by Signor Manfredini. Someday these ornaments will serve to enhance, gain admiration, and delight the hearer, in the splendor of our singing; but in the mouths of such as sing today they are so boring that one cannot listen to them without difficulty.

A voice which is not well-directed in its first years, and takes on vices, is not so easily cured of them as one thinks.

Fortified with the dreadful consequences of many examples, it is to be hoped that modern masters will hasten to imitate the example of the old schools, because we have observed that they were exact in their direction, and helpful to the voices.

It used to be said in the past that if the trill was not given by nature, one could not acquire it by art. I do not deny this; but let me say that the ancient masters did not leave any voice; agile by nature, imperfect, as we see in our own times; thus it is that we see on many occasions that they had recourse (whatever obstacles they encountered) to industry, an endless and indefatigable diligent patience, in using the most valuable aids in helping their scholars attain this end. This same insinuation is proposed by Pierfrancesco Tosi, as we will see in its place. I shall say nevertheless, that whoever possesses a perfect trill, can produce it and place it in the just positions, and keep it quiet in other situations to which it does not belong; he who does not possess it, not only lacks something in itself but also prejudices his singing in general.

I shall go ahead and reason on this proposition, to enlighten the studious youth how to obtain it through application, I repeat . . .

[B] Thus this proposition is true, and these same singers, in jest, have called the trill the "Allurement of singing," because no matter in what manner one may wish to employ it, it serves to freshen and adapt to the singing.

[C] I repeat this passage from the first edition, because I find it so necessary, useful and interesting. Imagine my great surprise to find it taken to task by Signor Manfredini in his work already cited. Certainly I do not wish to reform nature, even when she is avaricious and miserly with her gifts; but wherever she has given some disposition, no matter how slight, it seems to me to be advantageous and indispensable; not without guilt could I have passed over teaching a thing from which the profession reaps such lustre and success, as my constant experience has taught me; and I call upon others, and the common sense of everyone.

He goes on at page seven to say, ". . . that the trill must be natural, natural and then natural. To say that the trill is the most interesting quality of music is to increase its merit beyond its worth. The singing of portamento, the firmness of the voice, the flowing of it, the drawing out of it, the softening [*smorzarla*] of it at the right place and time, etc., are the true beauties of singing, and the trill is only an ornament, which does well when it is natural in a cadenza, and in some few places; but one can use it much less. Many times I have heard singing to the heart, without its having included the execution of a trill!"

What can I say after a decision made so outside of reason? I shall say only, that the more one lives, the more one hears. I suggest to all this, speaking respectfully, that never in all my days have I heard it suggest that "the trill is not the most interesting quality of vocal music, that is only an increase of its merit beyond its worth."

This absolute decision seems to affect the whole of the profession, not one single part of it. Had Signor Manfredini read my book with the necessary reflection, surely he would have observed, that I laid stress (out of a sense of duty) on those points which direct one into the path of fixing the voice, how to acquire the portamento; the art of knowing how to fix the voice, to make it flow, to spin it out, and reduce it, etc., etc., and why? Who does not know that all these things are necessary to a voice, and that they should be united for the formation of perfect singing? Thus it was necessary for Signor Manfredini to make another explanation, going ahead, although after the proposition, and saying: "How many times have I heard singing to the heart, without hearing a trill?" He could just as well have said, this quality of voice and singing shines brilliantly in the place where sinners gather for eight days to hear spiritual exercises; and above all else this makes an extraordinary effect after a sermon on the last judgement, because a poor voice, languishing and naked, can make the tears of sinners flow in great torrents, and move to great sorrow anyone whose heart has been excited and disposed to meditation on pathetic objects. Had he said this, he would have spoken very well indeed; but, according to me, such a voice will never be suitable for a theater, because in the scene it will need at the proper time the solidity, the spinning, the sudden decrescendo of the voice. . . and then these should be united to brio, agility of the voice, vibrato [*vibrare*], detached notes [*distaccare*], the drawing back [*ritirare*], strength, and appropriateness of expression, etc., in sum a perfect complexity of such varied things by which the artist, who assumes the burden of a principal part, is in a position to gain success in any character whatever.

Thus it is not for fear of any damage which the criticism of Signor Manfredini might be able to do me before the true professors, who know, that I have taken the trouble to justify and clarify my own opinion regarding the trill; but rather because I have a reasonable fear that the profession might suffer a disadvantage from the many inexpert masters who might let themselves be seduced by the words of Signor Manfredini and would neglect to cultivate the trill in those very voices where sufficient agility to do so is found.

[D] Footnote: I speak of these voices, and maintain that the masters should not neglect nor abandon them; and if Signor Manfredini had better considered my proposition, he would surely not have tried to assail it with so ill-supported reasoning.

[E] Insert Figure]3.

[F] When one falls into the minor mode, the studious youth will see that it falls upon the keys of the harpsichord which are but a half-tone apart.

[G] Insert Figure 14

[H] Insert Figure 15

[I] This example is inserted in the body of the text in the edition of 1774 and in the table of examples as Figure 16 in the edition of 1777.

[J] To render the voice apt to every kind of execution, one should exercise it by making the gruppetto inverted. See Figure 17.

[K] Insert Figure 18

[L] This ornament of singing, aside from the perfection of its execution, carries with it a just measure which each singer should give it in every place where he wishes to use it.

From this comes the rule that he who departs from natural usage passes from pleasure into annoyance. Above all else the young singer should avoid exercising and studies *sotto voce*, because not only the trill, but every other ornament of singing, more and more, when sung *sotto voce*, makes it impossible to execute them any other way, and every time that he wishes to produce them in full voice, huge in large and vast places, he cannot execute these passages, or if he execute them, they cannot be other than full of imperfections, and unpleasant. While it is easy to execute any ornament in a weak and soft voice, it is very difficult to execute them with a large and strong voice.

[M] . . .: in the case where the voice is required to sing with wind instruments such as the oboe and the trumpet, then in the final cadenza the long trill will be heard with great pleasure, because the strength of the chest, the art and ingenuity of the two artists can be observed.

[N] A voice which is sufficient for executing the trill with perfection will be able to execute the cadenza set forth in Figure 19.

On the contrary a well-directed voice, rich in low and high notes, sufficiently agile, but deprived of the trill, will execute all of the cadenza very well except for the scaletta of the ascending trill. Such a voice can demonstrate its strength and art, sustain the long notes, leap perfectly from the low to the high notes, and come forth with exactness in the cadenza; but all of this notwithstanding, the execution will remain imperfect, languid and pleasing to no one, because in this case the ascending trill is that which characterizes, perfects and gives the true value to the cadenza.

[A] The second and third paragraphs are changed as follows:

Before I go on, I should tell you that singers are of two opinions as regards cadenzas. The first is that the cadenza should be prepared with a graduated note, that is a *messa di voce*; and what follows should be an epilogue to the aria, or other composition, and made up solely of the figures and passages of which it is composed, which should be well-distributed, imitated and sustained in one single breath, the whole accompanied by the customary trill.

The other opinion is that the cadenza should be arbitrarily constructed by the singer, so that he makes the most of varied passages and stylized figurations, to the end of showing off the velocity and ability of his voice and himself.

Have no doubt that the first opinion is the better, and coherent with reason, being no more than an epilogue to the aria. The second is more convenient to the singer, because he can suffocate with the surprising quantity of notes made for the occasion, bring out the admiration of his listeners, who always remain surprised by the quantity of notes, and can be led away from reason and quality.

From this arises the fact that the young think nothing serves them better in the whole realm of art, than a cadenza.

I know that many believe this to be so, but I know better, that they fool themselves very greatly: and I do not blush to assert that the cadenza is one of the most scabrous and thorny parts of vocal music; in order to arrive at a perfect formation without defects, one must wish to overcome many difficulties. In order to understand that I speak the truth, it is enough to consider how often one hears a perfectly wrought cadenza. All of these necessary things I shall now proceed to enumerate exactly.

ARTICLE XII

[A] This is changed to read: The reflections which I have given up to this point are adaptable to those voices in which one finds a natural aptitude for singing.

[B] This replaces the second part of the first paragraph:

There are some, however, as I said in Article X, who are apt only to expression and thus are more or less restricted to singing notes and words [*note e parole*]. For such voices one should not pretend to be able even through study, to help them to the acquisition of the ornaments of singing, that is to say the trill and mordent, and finally to conceive gruppetti, nor others, because they lack all disposition completely.

A shrewd master in such circumstances should not only encourage the natural disposition, but also attentively insure that the voice in general is well in tune and "registered" with proportionate study. Then if one finds a natural grace in these voices, whatever it is, it should be cultivated and perfected, etc.

The voice gifted by nature with agility is the one which I wish to discuss in thie Article.

[C] These paragraphs are moved to the end of the Article, and the following sections take their place: One should be advised, that this study should not be undertaken until the master has succeeded in uniting the divided registers of the voice, as was said in Article VIII. If this essential point is overlooked, the voice will suffer not a little detriment, because in this condition of separation, the passage will be unequal, and consequently defective, as much in the strength and the clarity of the voice, as in the proportion and unity of it.

Every wise and diligent master is obliged to know, that in every voice, however poor and restricted, if it have a disposition for agility, he can find a style suitable for it, which can be produced naturally.

The whole difficulty lies in knowing the way to discover it, in order to put into practice all the means which are necessary for developing, polishing and loosening a voice not perfectly formed.

I shall not finish soon, if I wish to explain part by part the diverse qualities of passages, which lie beneath the art. I should say nevertheless, that among these are some easy and natural, and some difficult and scabrous. It is the duty of the master to choose among these that style which is most fitting for his student's ability, so that it may be reduced to perfection by appropriate and intensive study. I should add to the proposal, that there are some voices which are apt for ascending the little scales in leaps of thirds (Fig. 20), but are lazy and reluctant in descending; others show themselves easy in singing in descending motion, and difficult in singing by ascending motion. And it may also turn out that these same voices are also lazy and not apt for the execution of a passage formed of three, or even six notes (Fig. 21). Given such a case, that the master should wish to lead this voice to the execution of this new style at full force: I am of the opinion that such a voice would suffer a most noticeable damage, because forced into a style not natural to itself; and if the master, thus inexpert, believes that he can succeed through the continuation of such study; I shall say that he fools himself in this case, and the poor scholar, after such a long and irregular effort, will find himself rendered breathless, and unable to undertake any other study.

Thus it is necessary for the master to be a true expert in knowing the nature of each of his scholars, that he may with just caution lead them little by little, in whatever way is right for each voice.

One should not abandon or overlook that voice which is lazy in descending the divided scaletta, and equal attention should be given the other, which shows itself reluctant in ascending. All obstacles may be overcome through the medium of an appropriate daily study, and the master should change solfeggios, or even mix the passages with other excerpts which are related. With this methodical study, the master can succeed in solidifying, establishing, and loosening step by step, any voice.

Equal regulation should be used with the student who shows himself inclined toward easy execution of the passage in three and six notes; and if the master knows how to follow up and develop this voice, he will find it apt and pleasing in many styles, by which means the master can establish in this voice a varied style, free and vivacious, which rendered perfect, will be truly surprising: it is necessary that this voice acquire a perfect trill and mordent, that it may intensify, ornament and vitalize whatever song (a not slight gift) so that the ornaments are given with judicious attention to the place, so that they do not destroy the taste of the cantilena, and do not betray the sentiment of the words.

The *volatina* should be considered with agility of the voice. Every scholar, however mediocre in agility, should use all his attention to acquire this to perfection.

I should say, to explain myself with the utmost clarity, that this divides itself, and is executed, into two types: the first with motion (1) upward (Fig. 22), the second with motion downward (Fig. 23): one should know that both of these when they do not exceed the limits of the octave, are called *volatina semplice:* the other is called redoubled [*raddoppiato*] when it exceeds this limit (Fig. 24).

Among the multitude of passages and runs which are suggested by art, I esteem this above others, because it unites perfectly with vivacious cantilena, and miraculously also with the sustained style. If one wishes to see how many diverse ways it may be adapted for use, we see that it can serve to ornament a held note with a fermata, whenever it is done simply and smoothly; and he who wishes to ornament this note further, has only to add a trill, sustained and fixed on the note which ends the octave (Fig. 25).

And more, when the *volatina* (although simple) is done
with just proportion, it can tie, or give motion, and vivacity to a passage which follows, in both vivacious and sustained tempos. It gives extraordinary vitality when it is
adapted to a cadenza which finishes in strict time, that is,
the multiple *volatina*: all of this consists in knowing how
to redouble and graduate, so that it finishes proportionately
in the tempo.

Now one should examine what rule must be followed, so
that he attains perfection in every style to which he wishes
to adapt it. Without doubt one should believe that the *volatina* has much use with the *messa di voce*: and in fact, anyone who wishes to use it according to the rules, should produce the breath gradually, to expand the voice while still
holding the first note, which prepares it, and without doing
violence to the voice, should equalize and make the breath
light at the same time that he executes the *scaletta*, giving
only so much as will be sufficient for leading it gradually
to its end. This is called the *volatina* prepared with the
messa di voce. We have another, either the simple or redoubled, which is mixed with other passages in strict tempo, but
these should always be given with distinctness and gradation.
One should add to this that once undertaken, it should not
be interrupted, but should be lead to its final note all in
the breath. Commonly everyone thinks that the *volatina* should
be solid and sung as fast as possible, and I subscribe to this
same opinion, as long as the execution is without defect.

Although the rules of this art are clear and ratified
by the most expert singers, some, because they are ignorant
of knowing how to sustain the first note with the strength
of the chest, know even less the art of softly graduating the
breath; and when it happens that these take the first note
inconsiderately with violence, and not being in a condition
to be able to regulate it, believe that the only solution is
to tighten the fauces. The voice, in this irregular position,
cannot be other than defective and heavy, because it is shut
into the throat, and what little remains sounds as though it
were suffocated by the palate, and the *volatina* is transform-
ed into an ugly stricture of the voice, which in the end
arouses only compassion and annoyance in the listener.

In conclusion one should say that the *volatina*, and all
agility singing, should be sustained by the robustness of the
chest, and accompanied by the gradation of the breath, the
light action of the fauces, so that every note is heard distinctly, even when executed with the greatest celerity. Every
scholar should know that this study requires a given length of
time to acquire it perfectly, and also an untiring effort that
it be not left imperfect. This time and effort will not have

been spent in vain, but will serve to form a varied singing style, virtuoso, and in consequence distinct and sublime.

We can also be assured that a voice gifted with perfect intonation and mediocre agility, can yield, through appropriate study, to ascending and descending a *scaletta* composed of semitones (Fig. 26). The master, uncovering sufficient capacity in his scholar, should not delay to start him on this road, exercising him with a tranquil solfeggio, so that he may intone each monosyllable distinctly. This study requires patience from the master, that he may achieve perfection in a style which is difficult for him, because it requires a long and assiduous study, to overcome the difficulties which he is, of necessity, going to encounter. This passage, although executed with slow motion, should not be abandoned to being sung with a languid voice; but rather he should sustain the intonation and the voice on the right pitch, that he may mark sensibly each pitch with piano and forte, in order to render it perfect from the first note to the last. Thus this passage, executed with such precision, can make the conduct of a worthy master known and distinguished, and beside this can procure a particular credit for his scholar.

This passage ends at: "I have already spoken of the natural agility."

---

(1) *Remember that every note which marks the seventh in ascending, should be given slightly sharp by the voice, but this same note in descending should be given with naturalness of intonation.*

[D] Insert Fig. 27

[E] Mancini adds Faustina Hasse.

[F] The other style is called *arpeggiato* (Fig. 28) (*arpeggiato* because such a combination of tones of a chord, executed one after the other, is often practiced upon the harp, from which it derives the name of *arpeggio*).

The master should not pretend with his scholar, although he finds in him easy execution of all other kinds of agility, that he may put him on the road to this most difficult style, which requires a natural disposition, a voice perfectly in tune, and purged of every tiny defect, without which prerogatives he should not undertake the obligation. Natural disposition consists in possession of extraordinary lightness of the fauces, that the passage may be executed with the just amount of velocity.

Encountering a voice with this gift, the master should exercise it daily with a solfeggio, which should include a few measures of such passages, passing from the notes of the chest to the head, so that with continual exercise he may form

127

a perfect and light mixture of the voice. At the onset of this study the master should not only be cautious in the quality, but also quite discreet with the scholar, that every note be in tune, and that the speed of the tempo be moderate, that the scholar may continue this study insensibly without pain. It is easy for the master to know when he is ready to increase the tempo; and for this he should advance step by step, in order not to tire the chest. One should not believe that this cantilena requires detaching the note, since according to me, I believe it to be perfect when the voice marks the first note with discreet proportion, and ties the other three which follow; then the passage will be perfectly executed, according to the movement of the cantilena, and piano and forte can be distinguished, so necessary for the mixing of this passage. It is necessary not to destroy the cantilena by taking breath, because its perfection is procured by the union of the breath itself; not doing it in this way, it will remain prejudiced, if it is interrupted.

One should attend with care to accustoming the chest and the fauces to this extraordinary effort, so that the scholar, possessed of all these gifts, can appear before the public with a style so individual, that he will reap universal admiration and esteem.

[G] Insert Figure 29

[H] Add: . . . and if the notes descend from the high to the low, they should pass from high to low tying the voice with perfect gradation.

[I] Insert Figure 30

[J] I do not wish to fail to mention a defect I have observed in various singers, who often on low and bass notes tighten and shut the lips, and on the high notes open the mouth as much as possible, from which it arises that the low and high notes seem to be of two distinct characters, as one as bad as the other. The singer should endeavor to avoid this vice, which produces a bad effect on the listener.

[K] See [C]

[L] Some deceive themselves into thinking that they gain esteem by beating all the notes with immeasurable force, and making the voice unequal; and thus it happens, that they execute the passage all in one piece, without distinction, and in consequence deprive themselves of the grace which comes only from taking back, and giving the voice gradually, from which results a pleasing and perfect execution: from this caricature they resemble the rude and disgusting song of the turkey-cock; thus the professors vulgarly say that so-and-so sings like a turkey-cock [*sgallinacciano*]; others, finally, beside the defects already given use a motion of the tongue, supposing that this makes their execution easier.

Such a resource is completely prohibited by art, for the continual motion of the tongue does not allow the fixing of the alloted vowel, but carries with it an admixture of other vowels, which render the passage of necessity imperfect and the singer ridiculous.

Every scholar should know, therefore, in order not to err, that the beauty of every style of passage, to be well-executed, consists in perfect intonation of every note which composes it; by necessity, the perfect position of the mouth must be joined to this, and the tongue must rest quietly in the act of executing the passage. And what I say is true, as the best professors take great trouble to fold, or make a small channel in the middle of the tongue, so that the voice will find no impediment in coming forth. To all of this should be added the light motion of the fauces; and care to accustom the chest to regulate the voice, from its beginning to its end.

Through the means of study, the voice can be put into the state of doing any passage in sustained style; it is rendered agile by execution in vivacious movement, and in consequence it becomes easy to solidify and sound any note, if the cantilena requires, and thus the voice is equalized, and can be taken to the fastest motion, and one will become the possessor of that other gift of coloring every passage with piano and forte, so necessary to give just graduation and expression.

ARTICLE XIII

[A] Add: . . . and above all an exact, clear and perfect pronunciation of the words, not in the least exaggerated.

I recall the diligence and the study which the celebrated Pistocchi made in teaching his students, so that their pronunciation might be perfect, from which it arose that they could make every word heard to the listener, by making a distinction, where it occurred, between redoubled letters, as two *tt*, two *rr*, two *ss*, etc.

[B] Add Grammar

[C] Add . . . commonly called gutteral [*gorgia*].

ARTICLE XIV

[A] Mancini's list reads: Alessandro Scarlatti, Bononcini, Gasparini, Francesco Mancini, Domenico Sarro, Federico

Hendel [sic], Francesco Durante, and other equally famous men.

[B] This reads: Take into consideration those of Giovanni Hasse, Baldassare Galuppi, called Buranello, Niccolo Jommella [sic], Gaetano Latilla, Pasquale Cafar, Davide Perez, Gennaro Manna, Tommaso Trajetta, Niccola Piccinni, Antonio Salieri, Reichart [sic], Giovanni Cristiano Bach, Antonio Mazzoni of Bologna, Pitro Guglielmi, Amadeo Naumann, Misliweozek, Pasquale Anfossi, Giovanni Paiesiello, Carlo Monza, Tozzi, Borroni, Bertoni, Giambattista Borghi, Tommaso Giordano, and of Floriano Gasmann, lately dead, who beside his praiseworthy service to the Imperial Court, has left excellent works, and even more excellent scholars, among whom shines with distinction Antonio Salieri, *virtuoso di Camera* of the Imperial Court.

[C] Footnote: The noble Signora Marianna Martinex of Vienna has made the most authentic and just eulogy of this celebrated master. This incomparable lady, born with a superior genius for music, received its elements and perfection from the previously praised Signor Bonno. They were such, and her progress with them so great, that in a brief time she became the object of admiration of all the most famous masters of music. Her compositions were much in demand, and applauded in Naples, in Bologna, and in many other of the most renowned cities in Italy. I heard her myself, when she was still of tender years, sing, and play the harpsichord with surprising mastery, accompanying her singing, and expressing with great strength the musical meter, that the Signor Abbate Metastasio was inspired with much of that emotion which he realized how to excite in the human heart in his as yet unwritten works. Then the most celebrated Padre Martini, upon unanimous acclamation, was pleased to add to our *Accademia Filarmonica di Bologna*, this personage who, although a dilettante, could with just title call herself a great mistress, and rare genius of music.

[D] Let us look also at the works of Cavaliere Cristoforo Gluck, lately in the service of the Imperial Court, whose most penetrating vast genius and creative talent, is not only in possession of the most profound arcanities and recondite illuminations of philosophy and other sciences, but has developed a sense of the immensity thereof, from which rare, noble, interesting and sublime music was born, particularly French, of which he was the reformer, or, better, the autocrat. What can I say of such merit? What lustre can my weak voice add to his glory and fame, who not only in his native land, but throughout all the corners of Europe, lives immortally, and is venerated as the high priest of music? What more can be said, when one recalls that the composer of

130

Orfeo, Ifigenia, Alceste, and of *Paride ed Elena* has reaped
the applause of the French nation, so jealous of the glory
of her sons, and severest critic of the offerings of strang-
ers, and who has raised a bust in his honor in the midst of
the XVIII century? (1)

---

(1) *I will not extend myself by mentioning the many others
who still merit distinction, in order not to depart too far
from my subject, and since they are all well-known everywhere.
In fact, who can ignore the worth of a Wagenseil, whom the
Imperial Court lost on the first of March 1777? Or Giuseppe
Staffani, still in the Imperial service, who is, without
question, the best player of the harpsichord in Europe.*

[E] Add: La Merighi was also of this character.
[F] Add . . . invented by Giacomo Peri around the year
1600.
[G] Insert Figure 31. Add: I should advise, at this
place, that we have two accents, of which the one is called
the held-back [*trattenuto*], as in the exclamation, Oh God!,
the second unconstrained [*sciolto*], which is now languid, now
hastened, now serious and sustained, according to the diverse
emotions it expresses. The virtue of the master and the scholar consists in knowing them, and how to use them.

ARTICLE XV

[A] Add here the following: Vienna in Austria, 3 May
1777.
[B] A Table of Contents is added in this edition at the
end of this Article.

The letter below, without signature, appears to be in
the hand of Padre Giambattista Mancini:
My dearest friend:
You ask me and my weak knowledge whether you should reprint your book entitled *Pensieri e Riflessione pratiche sopra
il Canto figurato,* which was printed in Vienna in 1774. But
how can I criticize your thoughts, when among the many books
of music which pass before my eyes, I have found so few particularly on the subject of singing, which are so exact, so
instructive, so penetrating as your own? I have only observed *The Philosophical Discourses of Giovanni Camillo Maffei,*
of Solofra (*i Discorsi filosofici di Gio. Camillo Maffei da*

131

Solofra), in which is found a *Discourse on the Voice and the Method of Learning to Sing Agility, or Agility and Passages (Discorso della Voce e del Modo d'apparare di cantar Garganta, o sia di Gorga e di Passaggi)* Naples, 1562. I have also seen *The Opinions of Ancient and Modern Singers, or Observations on Figured Singing by Pierfrancesco Tosi (Opinioni de'Cantori Antichi e Moderni o Sieno Osservatzioni sopra il Canto figurato di Pierfrancesco Tosi)*, Bologna 1723. Also there is a book entitled *Freedom in Singing (Liberta del Cantare)* Lucca 1752. The unknown author of this last book speaks more of various other matters than of singing. The book cited by Maffei, after making an anatomical description of how the voice is made, and discussing remedies for saving and rendering more perfect the voices of singers, contents himself with demonstrating and teaching the method of ornamenting the art of singing with passages, after the style of his time: it was written many years afterwards. Pierfrancesco Tosi was the first to write about the materials of singing, discussing the most essential parts of the art. I have discovered a copy annotated in his own hand, which indicates that he thought of re-printing it with some changes, to the end of changing some expressions, and adding some varied ideas made by the best professors of his time. It is not the same case with you, who to this time have not had any opposition which pointed up defects, or demanded changes in your book, but rather you have had the applause and approbation of all the professors and the happy sell-out of all the copies of the first edition, and it was a singular excellence in the course of only two years to find the book translated into the French language, and printed in that Realm. If you are determined to reprint out of consideration for all those who would have desired to possess it, with the addition of some new observations, and advice, it would demonstrate that you are doing this for no other end than to please the profession, and make it useful to the public. A singular excellence which I found in your work is that singing is most difficult of all the arts to explain and teach without the living voice, and yet you have not failed to use all study and all diligence in the strength of your rules, precepts, and advice, and demonstrated all the defects which can occur, to impress the minds of young singers, (and I should say also Singing Masters) how necessary it is to learn this art in all precision, in which all youths can perfect themselves more by listening and observing the most celebrated singers of out times. Resolve yourself then hastily, my dearest friend, to publish the new edition of your book, to which you have added some new advice, and do not doubt that you will be forever welcomed and universally applauded, especially by the professors of singing.

From the reference to the French edition, it can be assumed that this letter was written about 1776; not later than
the appearance of Manfredini's *Regole armoniche,* however, for
the writer apparently does not know of Manfredini's attack
on Mancini.

Esemplare

prima ottava   seconda ottava

Do Re Mi Fa Sol Re Mi Fa Re Mi Fa Sol Re Mi Fa

Figura 1ᵃ

2. Tuono di ut
    Diesis
    terza mag. re
    pa   ut   pa

3. Tuono di re
    B - molle
    terza mag. re
    pa   ut   pa

4. Ut Diesis
    pa   tu.

5. Re B-molle
    pa   tu

133a

Esemplare

Figura

133b

133c

Figura   Esemplare

20.

21.

22.

23.

24.

25.

26.

adagio

volatina simplice

volatina raddopiata

adagio

133d

Esemplare

Figura

27. andante

28. Allegro / Allegro

29. Andante

30. Allegro / Adagio

31. onde mai tu vedesti

133e

APPENDIX II

GLOSSARY OF TECHNICAL TERMS

I have endeavored to find the broadest possible defini-
tion of certain technical terms Mancini used, and to explain
them in enough depth to give a reasonable idea of the thought
which Mancini was attempting to express. Some of these we
can only guess at, basing our surmise upon contemporary reports of what singers did in this and that case. The thing
which we must avoid at all costs is considering the art of
singing, as practiced in the eighteenth century, to have con-
sisted in anyway in singing softly and delicately, at the expense of expression and volume of sound. Volume was not an
end, as it has become in our day, but a by-product of the
perfect technical accomplishments of the greatest singers of
a great era. Coloratura singing was demanded of everyone;
but this is not exclusive of breadth and nobility of tone,
as we have seen in our own time in the singing of certain
dramatic artists. Battistini, DeLuca, Callas, Sutherland,
Caballe, and Horne all had or have, sufficient volume without
sacrificing clarity and brilliance of coloratura passages.
What vanity leads us to believe this an accomplishment of our
own time, rather than a return to earlier virtues? Word
values, brilliant diction and enunciation, are hallmarks of
the eighteenth century; as for volume, let us remember that
less volume is required to balance an orchestra, acoustically
speaking, in a large hall than in a small hall, where the
sound of the instruments may be enhanced by the closeness of
the walls. The physiology of the castrato tended to give
more sheer size to the artificial soprano than to the real
soprano; and of course there must have been the same percen-
tage of vocal phenomena in the eighteenth century as we find
today.

APPANNATA: Dim, dull, or hoarse. A voice may be said to be
  appannata when it has a slight thickness or veil on it,
  from nature.
CALATO: See under *TRILL*
CANTABILE: Literally, singing. Mancini uses it in two sen-
  ses, one the modern one of a lyrically legato aria or
  phrase, the other simply to signify the ordinary flowing
  phrase of the song. A *CANTABILE ARIA* is one in which the
  prime emphasis is placed upon the smooth delivery of the
  phrases, with ornamentation which does not destroy the calm
  mood. This is one of about eleven types of aria given by

134

sources as 'routine' types.

CAPRINO: See *TRILL*

CAVALLINO: See *TRILL*

CHIAROSCURO: A term taken over from the art of painting, where the modeling is done by means of 'light and shade' rather than line. Thus, a voice which is capable at one and the same time of brilliance and depth.

COLASCIONE: Strained, in the sense of purified, filtered. Can also mean a flowing or fluid dripping.

CONDUR LA VOCE: In this case, I think Mancini means the bringing forth of the voice, literally, the leading of the voice from the throat, the production.

CRESCIUTO: See *TRILL*

DISTACCARE: Detached. This grew into staccato in the later period, and indicates a stopping of the tone, but not the phrase, or taking of breath, between notes.

GRUPPETTO: I have retained this term, which means literally 'a small group,' to indicate the four-note trill, which can be taken from above or below, as shown at a later date by Vaccai.

IMPASTO: Literally, 'paste.' Mancini meant here that kind of vocal production, or that kind of voice, which has a certain natural fullness, associated with a way of singing wherein the singer produces a tone of chiaroscuro quality, which has the richness associated with freedom of the throat and vocal apparatus, so that the tone is almost thick, but retains a clear point. Mancini uses it only in the sense of a vocal virtue, something to be developed and sought after by every singer, a reliable basic quality of "full-throatedness."

MARTELLATO: Literally, 'hammered.' The execution of ornaments in *martellato* style differs from staccato in that there is a certain amount of decrescendo in each *martellato*. Garcia, in *Hints on Singing*, discusses this more fully. Lamperti recognized several ways to do detached agility work, in his book *Theoretical Guide*.

MESSA DI VOCE: A vocal ornament, frequently used as a training device, wherein the voice is started at the softest possible level of intensity, swelled to the greatest possible volume, and reduced again to the softest. It was considered indispensable for long notes in slow tempi, as a device to retain intensity of expression. Redi, in *Bel Canto*, gives several different versions of this ornament/exercise.

MISTO DI GRANITO: This term gave me the most trouble of all. Buzzi in the edition of 1912, simply translates it as "mixture of granite." Delving more deeply into the question,

135

I wish to suggest that this is intended to describe the
solidity in performance of ornaments, passages, etc.,
which is characteristic of the voice with good breath-
support for the tone. Thus it becomes a "mixture of
granitic solidity," indicative of full-voice performance
of ornaments and embellishments, as distinct from those
which are easily thrown off in half-voice. There is an
additional overtone of rock-like solidity of tone in this
phrase, totally consistent with such others as *CHIAROSCURO*
and *IMPASTO*; the whole suggests the total participation
of the physical elements in singing, and brings back
Tosi's injunction to "let the voice issue forth free and
clear, neither passing through the nose, nor trapped in
the throat." What better description of free production
could there be?

MORDENTE: The *mordente* is properly nothing more than a note
below the 'real' note, sounded rapidly, and in the key;
thus, if in the key it is a half-tone, a half-tone is
sounded; if a whole-tone, a whole-tone is sounded. This
ornament is found in music of all periods, and is an in-
tegral feature of such a late *Lied* as Schubert's *Ihr Bild*.
In Bach's music this is used where he asks for a trill on
a short note.

MUSICO: This is an ambiguous term, reflecting the reserva-
tions which the eighteenth century held regarding the castrati. Often it is used to avoid the use of the bald terms
"*castrato*" and "*evirato*"; in these instances it definately
describes the castrated male. However, it is also used
simply to describe musical performers attached to a royal
or ecclesiastical household, although these are often vocal
performers. When a person is described as a *musico*, one
cannot be certain whether he was castrated or not.

NOTE E PAROLE: This is an early frame of reference for the
"patter aria," in which there is a note for each syllable,
and vice versa. Literally, 'notes and words,' to indicate
the absence of long florid sections.

PORTAMENTO: This term, which apparently first meant nothing
more than the bringing forth of the voice, came in later
years to indicate a certain super-legato in which *all* the
intervening notes between two distant notes were sounded,
giving a kind of exaggerated sliding effect. It is quite
effective when properly used; unfortunately it has become
a vice with singers whose musicianship is not up to dif-
ferentiating between clean and tied intervals, and it has
lost a considerable amount of its impact thereby.

RECITATIVO: Recitative was of two varieties, *Recitativo semplice*, and *Recitativo instrumentale*, or *stromentato*. The
semplice was accompanied only by the harpsichord and cello

136

continuo, and was quite free, being a heightened speech-form. The *instrumentale* is accompanied by other instruments, strings and/or winds, and is more dramatic, depending upon declamation and just accentuation of the text rather than the rapid patter of the semplice. All forms of musical declamation can be divided into these two, at some level; their use and differentiations easily seen in the *Barbiere di Seviglia* of Rossini.

RITIRARE: Mancini uses this in regard to the breath; his intention, I think, was to indicate the effortless re-filling of the lungs, in such places as 'taking and re-taking of the breath.' He also uses it in the sense of a sort of vocal *rinforzando*, which must be interpreted as a reinforcing of the tones by means of a vocal accent without breaking the phrase.

RUBAMENTO DI TEMPO: More commonly known today as *Tempo rubato*. The characteristic of this style which is usually over-looked is that the accompaniment, or in piano-playing, the left hand, continues in the original tempo, while the voice, or the right hand, plays with note values, to give a very vocal and free reading of the melodic line. The important thing is that the meter be kept going, so that the effect of 'robbery of the tempo' is heightened, rather than resorting merely to a series of ritards and accelerations. The first beat of each measure should be together; beyond that it is left to the genius of the performer and the accompanist to make the most lyrical and vocal freedom possible within this restriction.

SBALZARE: This apparently refers to singing in a style where leaps are features; a later example of this is found in the variations to "Son vergin vezosa," from Bellini's *I Puritani*, where Elvira is required to strike numerous notes that are an octave or such above the notes she has sung before. The idea in this kind of singing was to amaze the listener by taking high notes with clarity and brilliance.

SCIOLTO: Mancini intends here to convey the easy, loose and free throwing off of passages and phrases associated with good production, so that the singer does not equate physical exertion with good technique.

SCIVOLO: A sliding or gliding; or, in some cases, a trill. Mancini apparently intends to convey the idea of an exaggerated, and overused, *portamento*.

SMORZARLA: To shade by extinguishing. Mancini obviously intends a kind of "echo-tone" achieved by shutting, or nearly shutting, the mouth, to give a suffocated and closed tone to the voice in certain passages. It lies on the dark side of chiaroscuro, but is easily done if the interior position of the organs is not disturbed in closing the exterior, so that only a mild muffling is achieved; if too much covering is done, the tone will not carry.

SPIANARE: To level out, to make plain. Mancini intends here to convey the idea of a simple letting out of the voice, a "spinning out," in the sense that nothing is done to color or change the tone produced naturally and easily from a pure vowel. CANTO SPIANATO, then, is nothing more nor less than the simplest pouring-forth of the voice, without added coloration.

STRASCINO: The drawing out, or pulling out, of the voice, or of an interval. In the case of the voice, it simply means bringing the voice forth clearly, with the full weight of the breath behind it; in the case of an interval, it means giving the greatest measure of *portamento* to an interval, so that it is "dragged over." This is considered a vice today, because it is abused; in Mancini's day it was a legitimate ornament.

TRATTENUTO: Held back, as in time or in intensity. If a note is *trattenuto*, a slight retard is made, for emphasis. If the voice is *trattenuto*, then it is reduced in volume for coloristic purposes; usually it is made suddenly, for maximum effect, as in a sudden decrescendo.

TRILL: I have included here all the types of *trill* which Mancini discusses. He speaks of the CALATO: A diminishing trill, in which a decrescendo is made; CRESCIUTO: Increased, in which more volume and intensity are added, the reverse of the *calato*; CAPRINO: Which takes its name from the goat, and which is a defect which resembles the bleat of that animal; the CAVALLINO: Which takes its name from the horse, and resembles the neighing of that animal; and the RADDOPIATO: Which is, literally, 'redoubled,' indicating that it is left off by an ornament, and taken up again without a break for breath, before the final cadence.

VELATA: Literally, 'veiled.' This refers to a voice which has been given a certain rich dark quality by nature, of which Rosa Ponselle is the leading example in our own time. The veil is a product of nature, and cannot be removed without great damage to the voice; Giuditta Pasta had such a veil, and it is a considerable advantage to a dramatic singer, though absolutely destructive to one who has not got it by nature, and attempts to acquire it. Gracia's *Hints on Singing* has a good discussion of this question.

VIBRARE: Literally, simply 'to vibrate.' However, Mancini apparently intends something more by his use of the term, and I think that he meant to convey the idea of a voice which continues to resonate, or sound, a note, even when the pitch is carried to its end. In other words, a full sound, which retains its support and body to the end of a phrase.

VOLATINA: Literally, ' a little flight.' Specifically, a short run of notes, up or down, used either as an exercise in agility or as an ornament, filling in a passage of notes of greater intervals, to differentiate from a *portamento*, which is a 'dragging' of intervals. The *volatina* sounds all the intervals; the *portamento* subtly suggests the notes, but slides through them without stopping to define individual pitches.

APPENDIX III

BIOGRAPHICAL NOTES

Not all of the persons considered eminent enough for mention by Mancini have found their way into contemporary dictionaries or encyclopaedias. Even such early sources as Burney's *General History of Music*, and Fetis' *Biographie universelle des musiciens* fail to mention some singers and composers, or if they do mention, fail to give dates. And the dates given by Fetis, especially, are always open to discreet inquiry.

However, it has been felt best to include whatever information was available, trying to indicate scrupulously where it was conjectural; a single mention of a singer or a composer may lead a diligent researcher to concurrent searches and assist him in locating definitely one singer or composer among several of similar name. An interesting picture emerges from the attempt to locate this or that singer or composer among the multitudes plying their trades in the seventeenth and eighteenth centuries.

Most singers and composers will be found listed under their surnames; in the case of certain of them who gained extraordinary renown under assumed names, I have felt it better to list them under the name of their greatest renown. Thus, Carlo Broschi is listed under *Farinelli*; but *Appianino* under his surname, Appiani. If this is confusing to some, suffice it to say that the search for several of the persons hiding behind pseudonyms was not always easy.

AGUILLAR, Antonia Maria Girelli, fl. c. 1760-75. A soprano, she sang in Milan in 1771, in a serenata by Mozart for the wedding of Archduke Ferdinand. She sang in London in 1772-2, where Burney praised her style, but said her intonation and voice were past their prime, although she must have once been very good indeed.

AGUJARI, Lucrezia [la Bastardella], 1743-1783. A student of P. Lambertini; she made her debut in 1764 in Florence. In 1780 she married Giuseppe Colla. She possessed a phenomenal three octave range.

AMOREVOLE, Angiolo, 1716-1798. A tenor, he sang in London in 1741. Burney praises his taste and expression. He was one of the leading tenors of his day.

[Amadori] *TEDESCHI, Giovanni* fl. c. 1740-75. A tenor, he sang at Berlin in operas by Graun. He opened a singing school in Naples, but the date is not certain. Fetis has him confused with Giuseppe Amadori. He was among the great tenors of his age.

AMADORI, *Giuseppe*. A composer and teacher of singing. He opened a school of singing in Rome in the late 17th century. He is said by Eitner to have been a student of Bernacchi, but this is an obvious confusion with Tedeschi, who called himself Amadori.

ANFOSSI, *Pasquale*, 1727-97. An operatic composer and a student of Piccinni. He was very popular in London. He served as maestro at the Lateran from 1792 until his death.

ANIBALI, *Domenico (ANNIBALI)* c. 1700-79. A soprano castrato, he made his debut in Rome in 1725. He possessed an exceptionally high voice, reaching F *in alt*. He was a chamber singer in Dresden, 1729-64. He also sang in London from 1736.

APPIANI, *Giuseppe* [Appianino], 1712-1742. A contralto castrato, and a student of Porpora. He made his debut in Venice in 1731. He was extremely popular in major Italian cities.

APRILE, *Giuseppe*, 1738-1813. A contralto castrato who could sing soprano. Haböck gives his range as three octaves and a note, from b to C *in alt*. Aprile was the teacher of Cimarosa, Michael Kelly, and Manuel Garcia II. In 1791, he published, in London, *The Modern Italian Method of Singing*.

ASTORGA, *Emanuele Gioacchino Cesare Rincon, Baron d'*, 1680-1755 or 57. A celebrated composer who travelled extensively. He was praised as a singer and as a performer on the harpsichord. His most famous compositions are chamber cantatas.

ASTRUA, *Giovanna*, 1730-1757. She was prima donna in Naples, and in 1748 engaged in a famous dispute with Caffarelli. She was a student of G. F. Brivio.

BABBI, *Gregorio*. President de Brosses wrote that he was the one tenor that he heard in Italy with a high register comparable to that of the French tenor Jelyotte. Babbi is generally considered as one of the finest tenors of the 18th century. He is not to be confused with the tenor, Matteo Babbini, (1754-1816).

BACH, *Johann Christian*, 1735-1782. Known as the "London Bach", he was the eleventh son of J. S. Bach. He studied with his brother, K. P. E. Bach and Padre Martini. In 1762, he established himself in London where he was immensely popular. He influenced W. A. Mozart whom he met in London in 1764.

BALLERINI, *Francesco*, fl. c. 1690. He was one of the finest singers of his period. He sang in Mantua in 1690, and may well be the same 'Ballarini' [sic] who sang in the court of Joseph I of Rome. If that is so, then he died about 1700.

He is called in some sources, "Baron Ballerini."

BARTOLINO, Vincenzo of Faenza. Burney tells us that Bartolino sang in London from 1782-86, and that he was a soprano castrato. He died after 1792. Fetis lists a Bartholomeo Bartolini of Faenza, [c. 1685 - d. after 1730]. He was one of the greatest singers of the eighteenth century. He studied with Pistocchi and Bernacchi. He was in the service of the Elector of Bavaria, 1720-30. Obviously, this is neither the same man nor his father, but perhaps a relative.

BERNABEI, Gioseffo Antonio, 1649-1732. A composer; he studied with his father. He composed fourteen operas and much sacred music. He was maestro di cappella in Munich from 1688.

BERNACCHI, Antonio, 1685-1756. A soprano castrato and pupil of Pistocchi, he sang throughout Italy. In 1729, he sang in London in Handel's troupe. He founded the Bolognese School of Singing in 1736. Many famous singers numbered among his pupils.

BERNASCONI, Andrea, 1706-84. He was a celebrated composer and Kapell-Meister at Munich from 1755. He taught his step-daughter, Antonia, for whom Gluck wrote Alceste in 1767. She was noted more for her acting than for her singing.

BERTONI, Ferdinando Giuseppe, 1725-1813. A composer and pupil of Padre Martini. In 1752, he was appointed as organist of St. Mark's in Venice. From 1757-97, he taught at the Conservatorio dei Mendicanti. He visited London in 1780. Burney describes him as a man of ability and taste, but no genius.

BONNO, Giuseppe (BONO), 1710-88. A composer who studied at Naples. He succeeded Floriano Gassmann as Hofkapelmeister in Vienna, 1774. He is best known for his court compositions.

BONONCINI, Giovanni Battista (BUONONCINI), 1670-1755. A composer and most famous member of a long line of composers. In 1721 he went to London to assist Handel at the Royal Academy of Music. He was quite popular, but suffered from comparison to Handel, and about 1732, he moved to the court of Louis XV. He composed ca. 22 operas, including several at Vienna.

BONTEMPI, Giovanni Andrea Angelini, 1624-1705. Reputed to have been a soprano castrato, he was a student of Virgilio Mazzochi. In 1643, he was a leading singer at St. Mark's in Venice. In 1647, he went to Dresden, where he was associated with Heinrich Schütz. Here he produced the first Italian opera in Northern Europe, his own Il Paride, 1662, for which he wrote both the music and the libretto. It lasted from 9 P.M. to 2 A.M., and took in most of the Trojan War. Bontempi was by all accounts a most remarkable man, designing and staging his own works, writing history, both musical and economic. His *Istorica musica*, Perugia, 1695, is an extremely interesting work, from which many authors have quoted the section on the use of the echo.

BORDONI *Hasse, Faustina,* c. 1700-81. A mezzo-soprano, she studied with Gasparini and Benedetto Marcello. She made her debut in 1716 and went to Vienna in 1724. She spent 1726-28 in London and married J. A. Hasse in 1730. She was especially noted for hir agility and perfect intonation. She is considered one of the finest singers of her day.

BORGHI, *Giambattista (Giovanni Battista),* 1713(?)-96. A composer, he wrote approximately 20 operas and much church music.

BORRONI, *Antonio (BURONI, BORONI),* 1738-92. A composer and student of Padre Martini and G. Abos. He was primarily a court and church composer and he wrote 21 operas. He was Maestro di Cappella at St. Peter's in Rome from 1778-92.

BOSCHI, *Francesca Vanini,* fl. c. 1711. A contralto and wife of the Bass, Giuseppe Boschi. In 1711 she sang in London in Handel's *Rinaldo*.

BRIVIO, *Giuseppe Ferdinando.* He opened a singing school in Milan c. 1730, where his students included Visconti and Astrua. There is considerable confusion between G. F. Brivio and the castrato Carlo Francesco, who was the teacher of Appiani and Salimbeni. They may, indeed, have been the same man, or brothers.

BULGARELLI, *Maria Benti* [la Romanina], 1684-1734. A prima donna soprano and one of the most distinguished of early leading ladies. She made her debut in 1703, and sang at Venice as late as 1729. Her career was intertwined with that of Metastasio, whom she followed to Vienna in 1725. Her fame was widespread in Europe.

BURNEY, *Charles,* 1726-1814. An English musician and historian, he was a student of Dr. Arne. He received the Mus. Doc. from Oxford in 1769. Dr. Burney was the author of the *History of Music*, one of the first comprehensive attempts to write a history on the subject. In the course of gathering materials he travelled extensively on the Continent, and his notebooks on these journeys have been published and republished. The first volume of the *History* appeared in 1776. Burney wrote numerous other books concerning music, and was widely known in his day as a musical savant. His daughter, Fanny, has gained some renown as a diarist.

CAFARO, *Pasquale (CAFFARO),* 1706-87. A composer and patron of Caffarelli, to whom he taught the elements of music. He became maestro at the Chapel Royal of Naples and Director of the Conservatorio della Pieta.

[Caffarelli] MARJORANO, *Gaetano,* 1703-83. A soprano

castrato. He made his debut in Rome, 1726. He was one of
the greatest singers of his day and the leading rival of
Farinelli. Porpora was his teacher and considered him the
greatest singer he had even known. He sang throughout
Europe with the greatest success. The effect of his singing was sometimes offset by the shortcomings of his character.

CAMPEGGI, Francesco, fl. c. 1730. He was a teacher of
singing in Bologna, where he taught Tesi, who had been sent
to him by Redi. In 1719, he was elected to membership in
the Accademia Filarmonica of Bologna; in 1731, he was principal of that organization. He was organist at many of the
major churches in Bologna.

CARESTINI, Giovanni [Cusanini], 1705-1760. A soprano
castrato whose voice later became a deep contralto. A
student of Bernacchi, he made his debut in Rome in 1721. He
sang throughout Europe and from 1733-35 he was in England
with Handel's troupe. Burney remarked on his personal beauty
and the intelligence of his acting. He had a remarkably
florid technique.

CARLANI, Carlo, 1738, d. after 1780. A tenor, born in
Bologna, and a student of Bernacchi. Carlani was considered
among the greatest tenors of his age.

[Cavadenti] CASALI, Gaetano, d. 1792. Fetis lists a
Giambattista, or Giovanni Battista, Casali, maestro di cappella at San Giovanni in Laterano, 1759-92, who wrote several
operas. Campaspe was presented in Venice in 1740. He was
for a short time teacher of Gretry, but did not find any unusual talent in him and sent him away.

CICOGNANI, Giuseppe. Nothing can be found concerning
this singer apart from the facts that Mancini states. His
birthplace was Cesena.

CONCIALINI, Carlo, 1744-1812. A soprano castrato, he
made his debut in Venice. He became a member of the Bava-
rian court in 1763, and from 1770-80 was associated with the
court of Frederick II in Potsdam. He was especially noted
for the ability to swell a tone, and to trill. Gerber says
he was especially good in adagios.

CONSORTI, Salvatore, Born in Ascoli, he was a singer
at the Royal Chapel in Naples.

CONTI, Giovacchino [Gizziello], 1714-61. A soprano
castrato and student of Dominico Gizzi. He made his debut
in Rome in 1730. He seems to be the only singer that Caffarelli admired. He went to London in 1736 to join Handel's
troupe. He sang in Lisbon 1743-53. Burney admired the
pathos, delicacy and refinement of his style.

CORELLI, Arcangelo, 1653-1713. A violinist and composer. He studied with Benvenuti and Simonelli. He created

the concerto grosso and was well known and highly respected as a virtuoso and composer for violin, in the favor of Queen Cristina of Sweden, in Rome.

[Cortona] *CECCHI, Dominico* , c. 1660-1717. A castrato, he made his debut in Bologna in 1673. He sang in many of the leading courts of Europe, including München and Vienna. He was involved in many scandals because of his bad humor.

COTUMACCI, Carlo (CONTUMACCI), 1698-1775. A composer and organist; student of A. Scarlatti. The majority of his works are for the church.

CUZZONI, Francesca, c. 1700-1770. A soprano and student of Lanzi. She made her debut in Venice in 1719 and came to London in 1723 to join Handel's troupe. She attained great fame in London. About 1728 she sang in Vienna. Her intonation was perfect as was her agility. She had a compass of two octaves: c'-c'''.

DE AMICIS, Anna Lucia, c. 1740, d. after 1789. A soprano, said to have been a student of Vittoria Tesi. Known best for her ability to sing ascending staccato passages, reaching E *in alt*. She appeared in opera buffa at first, but her sweet voice and polished execution soon made her popular in opera seria. J. C. Bach wrote several pieces for her, in which she appeared in London.

DODDI, of Cortona. A canon of Cortona, whose fame rests entirely on his use of the system of solmization given by Mancini in Chapter V.

DURANTE, Frencesco, 1684-1755. A composer and teacher. Duni, Traejtta, Vinci, Jommelli, Piccinni, Guglielmi, Paisiello, and Pergolesi numbered among his students. The majority of his works are for the church. He is one of the founders of the "Neapolitan School."

EGIZIO, Domenico (GIZZI), 1684-1745. A teacher and singer, most noted for having been the teacher of Gizziello. He was himself a singer, and student of Pistocchi, Fago and Scarlatti. In 1720, he opened his class at San Onofrio, in Naples.

ELISI, Filippo, A tenor singer, not a castrato, as given by Heriot. He took the part of Eumene in a *pasticcio* of the same name in London, 1765, and appears before that in Lisbon in 1755, in Perez' opera, *Alessandro nell' Indie*. Burney mentions appearances in London in 1760, and praises him as a "great singer. . .still a greater actor," and says he had a wide range, and was fond of great leaps of fourteen or fifteen notes.

FABBRI, Annibale Pio (FABRI) [Balino] , 1697-1760. A tenor singer and student of Pistocchi. Fabbri was considered one of the leading tenors of his age, and was the favorite of the Emperor Charles VI. He was a member of the Accademia

Filarmonica of Bologna, and several times its Principal. He came to England in 1729 to join Handel's troupe. He enjoyed great success there through 1731. In later years, he served in the Royal Chapel in Lisbon, and died there.

FAGO, *Nicola* [Tarentino], 1676-1745. A composer who studied with Alessandro Scarlatti and Provenzale. Jommelli and L. Leo were among his students. He was the brother-in-law to the castrato Nicolini.

[Farinelli] BROSCHI, *Carlo*, 1705-82. A soprano castrato, pupil of Porpora and Bernacchi. Highly esteemed wherever he sang, Farinelli possessed unusual beauty of voice, taste and expression. He is reputed to have been a moving actor. He retired from the stage in 1737 to become the singer to Ferdinand VI of Spain, where he exercised considerable political power. He retired to Bologna in 1759, immensely wealthy. He seems to have been one of the most generous of castrati, and open in his admiration of other singers.

FEDI. Bontempi, in *Istoria musica, etc.*, Perugia 1695, gives a detailed description of this singing-master's attention to his students, and the great care he lavished upon them. He apparently opened the first school devoted exclusively to singing, in Rome, early in the seventeenth century, followed soon by Giuseppe Amadori. It is not inconceivable that this may be Francesco Maria Fede, born in Pistoia, early in the seventeenth century, and admitted to the Pontifical Chapel, 1667, as sopranist, then *maestro di cappella* at Santa Margarita in Trastevere, and known as a composer.

FENAROLI, *Federico Fedele*, 1730-1818. A composer and theorist, he studied with Durante and Leo. He counted Mercadante, Cimarosa and Zingarelli among his students. His theoretical writings were highly esteemed. The majority of his compositions were for church use.

FEO, *Francesco*, 1691-1761. A composer who studied with Fago. His first opera was performed in 1713. He was chiefly a composer of operas and the majority of his works were written for Naples. He is also reputed to have studied with Porpora and Gizzi [Egizio].

FERRI, *Baldassare*, 1610-80. A soprano castrato and the first international star. He spent the majority of his career in the service of the courts of Poland and Germany. Little is known of his career outside of this service, except that he is reputed to have visited London in 1669 or 1671, and Italy in 1643. His fame rests in large part on the eulogy in Bontempi's *Istoria Musica*, 1695.

FONTANA, *Agostino*, fl. c. 1750. He was a singer in the employ of the Court of Sardinia in 1750. He is a member of a large family of Fontanas who were noted as singers. He was born in Turin, and was a student of Pasi.

146

GABRIELLI, Caterina [La Coghetta], 1730-96. A soprano and student of Porpora, Gluck and Metastasio. She led a truly fabulous life, and her successes were wide-spread. She came to London in 1775. Burney says her voice was exceptionally sweet, though of light weight, and that she excelled in agility. She was an actress of uncommon attainments and extraordinary personal beauty. Her character was colorful, and her private life was not always above reproach.

GALLO, Pietro (GALLI), died after 1781. Eitner says that Pietro Galli was an alto singer, presumably castrato, at the Hofkapelle, Vienna, from May 1732, to 1781. Nothing else is known of him. This may or may not be Mancini's Gallo; probably not.

GALUPPI, Baldassare [il Buranello], 1706-85. A composer and pupil of Lotti. His operas were quite successful in England and he is especially noted for the comic operas written in collaboration with Carlo Goldoni. In 1762, he was made maestro di cappella at St. Mark's.

GASPARINI, Francesco Micaelangelo, of Lucca, 1668-1727. A composer of operas and church music. He studied with Corelli and Pasquini and taught B. Marcello, among others. Many of his approximately 32 operas were favorites on the London stage, and Burney gives accounts of several performances. His fame today rests upon a treatise on figured bass accompaniment.

GASSMAN, Floriano (Florian Leopold), 1723-74. A Bohemian born composer and student of Padre Martini. He became Kapellmeister in Vienna in 1772. Salieri was his student. Many of his operas and chamber works were extremely popular.

GIORDANO, Tommaso, c. 1733-1806. A composer and member of a famous family of composers and performers. His major activities centered around Dublin, where the majority of his operas, all apparently in English, were produced.

GLUCK, Christoph Willibald, Ritter von., 1714-87. A composer who is best known for his reforms of operatic structure. In works like Orfeo and Alceste, Gluck shifted emphasis from the vocal splendor of the castrati, to the dramatic validity of well-constructed theatrical experiences.

GOTI, Antonio. The only information on this singer is that given by Mancini - that he was born in Tuscany, and was the virtuoso da camera in the court of the Grand Duke in 1777.

GRANDVAL, Nicolas Ragot de, 1676-1753. A French composer, and essayist, who was attached for a time to a troupe of comedians, then became the parish organist in a Paris church. His son was a well-known actor at the Comédie Français.

GRASSI, Cecilia, 1746, died after 1782. A soprano and wife of J. C. Bach. She came to London in 1766. Burney praised her intonation and her power to please without surprising. She was succeeded by Girelli Aguilar in 1772.

GRECO, Gaetano, c. 1680. A composer and student of Alessandro Scarlatti. From 1717, he taught composition at Conservatorio dei Poveri, where Pergolesi, Durante and Vinci were his studnets.

GUADAGNI, Gaetano, c. 1725-1792. A contralto castrato, largely self-trained, who debuted in 1747. He came to London in 1748 and sang in the operas and oratorios of Handel. He sang in the *Messiah* and *Samson*, and created the role of Orfeo in Gluck's opera, Vienna 1762. His style was not florid enough to induce him to submerge the music in fioratura. In 1769, he returned to England where he did not succeed at first; he had added considerable range at the expense of quality. He retired to Padua where he died in penury.

GUARDUCCI, Tommaso, c. 1720, died after 1770. A castrato soprano who gained greatest success in England. He was a student of Bernacchi. He was noted for the simplicity and finish of his singing, rather than for powers of execution. He gained a great reputation for oratorio singing. He retired in 1769, and Burney visited him the following year.

GUGLIELMI, Pietro Alessandro, 1728-1804. A composer and student of Durante. His comic operas were quite popular throughout Europe. In 1767, he came to London, where he remained with great success until 1772. He became *maestro di cappella* of St. Peter's in the Vatican, in 1793. His son, Pietro Carlo, was also a composer, whose works had considerable success [c. 1763-1817].

HANDEL, Georg Frederic, 1685-1759. A composer of the first rank. Born in Germany, educated there and in Italy, and a resident of England from 1710, with excursions to the Continent. He was a student of A. Scarlatti. Handel's numerous works have been thoroughly evaluated in many biographies.

HASSE, Johann Adolphe, 1699-1783. A composer, called *Il Sassone* in Italy, where his music was beloved. He was a student of Porpora and studied composition with Scarlatti. He also sang as a tenor. Widely considered the leading composer of operas of his day, Hasse's meanuscripts were largely lost in the fire in his home in Dresden in 1760. He was married to the singer Faustina Bordoni.

HUBERT, Anton (UBERTI), [Porporino], 1697-1783. A soprano castrato, student of Porpora, whose name he assumed for theatrical purposes. He entered the service of Frederick II in 1741, and was greatly renowned for his singing of Italian operas in Germany. He was the teacher of Mme. Mara.

INSANGUINE, Giacomo Antonio Francesco Paolo Michele, [Monopoli], 1728-1795. A student of Cotumacci who became a composer, teacher and organist. He wrote approximately fifteen operas.

JOMMELLI, *Niccolo*, 1714-1774. A composer who studied
with Padre Mazillo. At the age of 23, he began to produce
operas with great success. He later studied with Padre Martini. He settled in Venice in 1743, and then moved to Vienna
in 1749. He became noted for Germanic influences in his works
which entered the common musical practices of his day. He
was called the 'Italian Gluck' for his attempts at reform of
the Neapolitan opera style.

LANZI, *Francesco Giuseppe (LANZA)*, died after 1812. A
singing teacher and composer who was born in Naples and later
published songs there in 1792. He then went to London, but
returned to Naples in 1812 to become the singing-master at
San Pietro. He was the father of the London-based singing
teacher, Gesualdo Lanza.

LATILLA, *Gaetano*, c. 1713-1789. A composer who studied
with Gizzi [Egizio]. His first opera was received with great
success in 1732. His operas, about 36 in number, were widely
successful.

LEIDNERIN, *Caterina,(SCHINDLERIN)*. Nothing can be found
about this singer.

LEIDNERIN, *Marianna*, *(SCHINDLER, SCHINDLERIN)*. A soprano
and student of Rauzzini. Burney says she was totally unfit-
ted for her position on the stage, and owed all her successes
to the machinations of her teacher, of whom she was an un-
worthy exemplar.

LEO, *Leonardo (Lionardo Oronzo Salvatore de Leo)*, 1694-
1744. A composer, and one of the founders of the Neapolitan
school. He was a student of Fago, and trained Pergolesi, Jommelli, Traetta, Piccinni, Sacchini, etc. His many operas and
oratorios were highly successful.

MANCINI, *Francesco*, 1679-1739. A composer of Neapolitan
origins. His opera *Hydaspes*, was one of the first given entirely in Italian in London, produced there in 1710. It is
of this performance that Steele speaks in his famous article
in the *Spectator*, marking the appearance of Nicolini in London.
There is no apparent relationship between Francesco and
Giambattista.

MANFREDINI, *Vincenzo*, 1737-99. A composer and son of
Francesco Manfredini, with whom he studied, in addition to
Perti and Fioroni. In 1758, he went to Russia, remaining un-
til 1769. In 1798, he returned to Russia where he died. His
Regole armoniche was published in 1795. He composed a few
operas and other works.

MANNA, *Gennaro (MANNI)*, 1721-88. A composer who studied
with Sant Onofrio in Naples. He was apparently quite well-
received in his day, and Burney met him on his famous journey
to Italy.

MANZUOLI, *Giovanni* [Succianoccioli], 1725-c.1782. A

soprano castrato who made his debut in 1748. He came to
London in 1764, where he was hailed as the best castrato since
Farinelli. Mozart received some singing lessons from him in
London, when Mozart was eight! In 1771, Manzuoli retired to
his estate near Florence, where he taught. One of his students, the soprano castrato Manzoletto [Monanni, Angelo], was
the choice of Gabrielli for her leading primo uomo; a choice
perhaps not dictated by his vocal abilities, which were
limited.

MARTINEZ, *Marianna (MARTINES)*, 1744-1812. A composer
and friend of Metastasio. She had lessons on the harpsichord
from the young Haydn, and in singing from Porpora. She was
a talented dilletante, friend of Mozart and she kept her home
open to artists. Burney praised her singing highly.

MARTINI, *Padre Giambattista*, 1706-84. A musical director
of the eighteenth century, he studied with his father, Padre
Predieri, and the castrato, Riccieri. He entered the Francis-
can Orders in 1722, setting up residence in Bologna in 1725.
Burney estimated Martini's library to contain 70,000 books.
Musicians and scientists sent him copies of everything they
wrote, and he was the mentor and guiding spirit for the majority of composers and performers of his day. The edition of
Mancini's *Pensieri* [1774] used for this translation appears
to have come from that library, as it bears Martini's name
on the title page.

[Matteucci], SASSANI, *Matteo*, c. 1667, died after 1735.
A soprano castrato whose singing was so beautiful that "cantare come Matteuccio" became a stock compliment. Little is
known of him before his sensational success in Naples in
1693. He was at least as insufferable personally as Caffarelli and Marchesi, insulting dukes, getting embroiled with
women, etc. He held a position of great importance in the
court of Carlos II of Spain around 1698, and appears to have
retired about 1708.

MAZZONI, *Antonio*, 1718, died after 1761. From Bologna,
a composer whose operas and sacred pieces were respected.
He spent most of his productive life in Russia, Sweden, and
Denmark.

MAZZANTI, *Ferdinando*. A composer and singer about whom
little is known besides what Burney records of him in his trip
to Italy. He occupied a position at Stuttgart shortly after
Burney met him. In 1790, some songs were published in London.
He seems, during Burney's visits, to have been a very popular
singer in Rome.

MERIGHI, *Antonia*. A contralto profundo, who appeared
on the London stage in Handel's works, 1729-1731, then again
in 1736 and 1738. Her voice apparently was so deep that
Burney refers to her as a 'counter-tenor.'

METASTASIO, Pietro Antonio Domenico Bonaventura, 1698-1782. A Poet and patron of musicians, Metastasio wrote many of the libretti that were set, time and again, during the eighteenth century. He was, himself, trained by Porpora, and was a close personal friend of Farinelli. All-in-all he wrote about 35 opera libretti, some of which were set as many as 60 times. Like Padre Martini, Metastasio looms like a giant in the eighteenth century. He spent the greater part of his life in Vienna as Court Poet to the Emperor (1730-82).

MILLICO, Giuseppe, 173--1802. A soprano castrato who first came to fame as the hero in Gluck's *Paride ed Elena,* Vienna 1769. He came to London in 1772, with Sacchini, and both were roundly criticized, but remained to overcome their critics and triumph. Burney says that Millico's voice came more from art than nature. Millico retired to Naples, where his compositions were favorably received. Garcia II, as late as 1894, quotes an ornamented passage used by Millico [*Hints on Singing*].

MINELLI, Giovanni Battista, 1687-1762. A contralto castrato and student of Pistocchi, he sang in Bologna at San Petronio in 1712 and Munich from 1722-24. He was apparently a member of minor religious orders.

MINGOTTI, Regina (nee Valentini), 1728-1807. A soprano, student of Porpora, and chief rival of Faustina Bordoni Hasse in Dresden. She sang in Farinelli's troupe in Spain from 1751-53, whence she came to London, remaining the first lady of that city through 1765. She then returned to Dresden. Her voice, style, and stage action were all highly praised, though they wanted somewhat in feminine grace and charm.

MISLIWEOZEK, Josef (MYSLIWECEK, MYSLIWECZEK), 1737-81. A Bohemian-born composer who studied with Pescetti. His first opera was performed in Venice in 1767, and was a great success. From this time on his fame was made, and his more than thirty operas and additional music were quite popular. He was Gabrielli's favorite composer. The Italians called him Venatorini or 'Il divino Boemo' in despair of pronouncing his proper name. Mozart held him in great respect. The renowned Abt Josef Vogler studied with him. His death was the result of his unbridled life.

MONTICELLI, Angelo Maria, 1715-58. A mezzo-soprano castrato who was attached to the Austrian court from 1733-50 and sang with great acclaim. He came to London in 1740, where he succeeded Farinelli in the public esteem. Burney praises his appearance and the sweetness of his voice, along with the good sense not to attempt anything he was not sure of doing well. He was considered a better actor than many of his contemporaries.

MONZA, Carlo, 1744-1801. A composer, student of Fioroni,

and *maestro di cappella* at the Cathedral in Milan. Brilliant
and well-educated for his time. Burney heard a mass by Monza
in 1770, and several operas were produced with success.

NAUMANN, *Amadeo (Johann Gottlieb)*, 1741-1801. A German-
born composer who studied with Tartini and Martini. He became court Kapellmeister in Dresden in 1776. He wrote a
large number of successful operas, oratorios, etc.

[Niccolini] GRIMALDI, *Nicolo*, [Nicolino, etc.], 1673-1732.
A soprano castrato who studied with Provenzale. Nicolini is
of particular interest as being the first castrato to sing in
public in London. He first appeared there in 1708, in Scarlatti's *Pirro e Demetrio*, the reaction to which Steele duly
recorded in the *Spectator*. Nicolini then appeared in *Alma-
hilde* and *Hydasepes*. In 1711, he appeared in the first Handel
work, *Rinaldo*, in London. Then he sang throughout Europe, to
the greatest acclaim. He was particularly admired for his
acting, even after his voice had begun to decline. His brother
Antonio-Maria Grimaldi, was a well-known tenor, and his sister
Caterina, married Fago [Il Tarantino].

NUCCI, *Bartolomeo, of Pescia*. No reference besides Mancini's has been located regarding this famous teacher of singing.

ORSINI, *Gaetano*, c. 1679-1750. A contralto castrato in
the service of the German court in Vienna from 1700 to 1740.
He was highly regarded by the German critics of the time, but
they had not the advantage of hearing the best castrati.
Nevertheless, Orsini remains one of the foremost castrati of
his time not engaged actively in theatrical performances.

PACCHIEROTTI, *Gasparo (PACCHIAROTTI)*, 1740-1821. A
soprano castrato, student of Bertoni, and the third of the
members of the latter day trio of Marchesi, Rubinelli, and
Pacchierotti who shone with the same brilliance as Farinelli
had before. Not gifted with a particularly pleasing appearance, Pacchierotti nevertheless reached the highest ranks in
the profession as a result of his technical accomplishments.
A famous quarrel broke out between Pacchierotti and Gabrielli,
resolved when the diffident Pacchierotti admitted his inferiority to Gabrielli; this unfounded sense of inferiority
was a constant factor in his career.

PAISIELLO, *Giovanni*, 1741-1816. A composer, he studied
with Durante, Cotumacci and Abos. His operas gained him
international repute. His *Barbiere di Siviglia* was eclipsed
by that of Rossini. Paisiello spent a number of years at
St. Petersburg, in the employ of Catherine the Great (1776-
1784). While a gifted composer, he seems to have been quite
petty in his relations with other musicians, and on occasion
stooped to intrigue to gain his own ends. He was a fertile
composer, producing about 100 operas, and about as many other

works in varied forms. He is often credited with being the
first to use the concerted finale.

PAITA, *Giovanni*. Known as 'the Ligurian Orfeo.' Paita
was a well-known tenor singer, according to Haböck. He was
reputed to have been a student of Pistocchi.

PASI, *Antonio*, 1697 or 1710-1770. A contralto castrato,
student of Pistocchi, expecially noted for his adagio singing and for the purity of his style in general.

PASQUINI, *Bernardo*, 1637-1710. A composer, student of
Vittorio and Cesti, and teacher of Gasparini and Durante.
He wrote several operas in addition to other works, and was
an important figure in operatic life in Rome.

PELI, *Francesco*, c. 1690, died after 1737. A singing
master in Modena who was counted among the first of his
profession. He was also a composer. He established his
singing school in Modena in the years 1715-1730. Then, he
became attached to the Court of the Elector of Bavaria (later
Emperor Charles VI). His opera *La Costanza in trionfo* was
produced at Munich in 1737.

PEREZ, *Davide*, 1711, died after 1780. A composer and
student of Gallo and Francesco Mancini. He was highly successful in his operatic compositions and was counted among
the first composers of his day. He visited England in 1755.
He spent most of his productive career in Lisbon where he
died, like Handel, blind and the victim of his excesses.

PERGOLESI, *Giovanni Battista*, 1710-36. A composer and
student of Greco, Durante and Feo, who produced his first
opera while still a student. His serious operas were successful, but his intermezzo, *La Serva Padrona*, opened the way
for opera buffa. It is one of the earliest works still in
the repertoire.

PERI, *Jacopo*, 1561-1633. A composer, student of Malvezzi
at Lucca, and court musician to the Medici. He is generally
credited with the first 'opera', the *Dramma per musica Dafne*,
1597. With Caccini, and the rest of the Camerata of Bardi,
Peri started that revolution in musical style which resulted
in opera. Peri was a trained singer.

PERUZZI, *Anna Maria* [la Perrucchierina]c. 1690, died
after 1746. A soprano and the wife of the singer Antonio
Peruzzi. She sang widely throughout Europe during the period
of Tesi's greatest fame, and was one of her leading rivals.
She was in Prague in 1725, and Bologna in 1746. Little else
is known of her.

PICCINI, *Niccola (PICCINNI)*, 1728-1800. A composer,
nephew of Latilla, and a student of Durante and Leo. Piccini
wrote 139 operas, plus numerous other works. His operas were
highly successful wherever performed, and in Paris they un-
wittingly precipitated the quarrel with Gluck. Piccini

regretted this, as he was of a peaceful nature, and had the highest regard for Gluck. His works are noted for the lightness and melodic charm of their arias. He was associated with France from his arrival in Paris 1776, to his death, in many roles, including that of teacher of singing at what was to become the Conservatoire.

PISTOCCHI, Francesco Antonio, 1659-1726. A soprano castrato and founder of the Bolognese school of singing. Pistocchi was a student of Padre Vastamiglia and B. Monari in singing, and Perti in composition. His first work was published when he was eight. He was an Oratorian priest, and although he appeared in public, was of a retiring disposition in general. About 1702, he founded the singing school in which he formed Bernacchi, Bertolino da Faenza, Minelli, Pio Fabbri, etc.

PORPORA, Niccolo (Nicola Antonio), 1686-1768. A composer, singer and teacher, he studied with Greco, Matteo Giordano, and Campanile. His first opera was produced in 1708. Porpora's greatest fame was as a teacher of singing, and he numbered among his most famous students Farinelli, Caffarelli, Salimbeni, Porporino, Gabrielli, etc. George Sand's novel, *Consuelo,* is a fictional account of his later days in Venice. His operas were immensely popular, and they are quite idiomatic for the vocal talents of his students. His personality seems to have interfered somewhat with the success of many of his ventures, and he died in bitterness and poverty at the end of a restless life. Authorities are divided on the question of vocal study by Haydn with Porpora, but there is no question that Haydn was Porpora's assistant and student in composition in Vienna.

POTENZA, Pasquale. A castrato soprano who sang first man parts in London, 1757-59, succeeded by Tenducci. Burney says he had more taste than voice.

RAAF, Antonio (RAAFF), 1714-97. A tenor singer, German-born, and student of Ferrandini and Bernacchi. His name is generally today associated with that of Mozart, who wrote the part of Idomeneo, and the concert aria *Se al labbro,* K. 295, for him. Aside from this association, which arose when Raaf was already in his sixties, he was generally esteemed among the first tenors of his day. Mozart was unimpressed when he first heard the 63-year-old tenor, but the next year in Paris, his reaction changed to overwhelming approval. From that time they were fast friends.

RAUZZINI, Venanzio, 1746-1810. A soprano castrato who made his debut in 1765. He arrived in London in 1774, and was a great success. His name is generally linked to Great Britain. His technique seems to have been limited, but his voice was good, and his acting admired. Mozart wrote the

Esultate motet for him and Rauzzini also took part in *Lucio Silla*, an early opera by Mozart. In his own right Rauzzini was a composer and teacher, and numbered among his students the tenors Kelly and Braham, the most famous tenor of his day. Many anecdotes are told of Rauzzini's life in England.

REDI, *Tomaso*, c. 1650-c. 1735. A composer and teacher of singing, *maestro di cappella* at S. Casa di Loretto, Rome for about forty years. Redi is known for a controversy with Padre Martini, but was also an important voice teacher, his most famous student being Siface [Grossi]. A second Redi, Francesco, is given as a teacher in Florence, who formed Vittoria Tesi-Tramontini. If there is a connection between these two, it has not yet been clarified. Grove says his singing school was established in Florence in 1706, which would argue against this being the same Redi as Tomaso.

REGGINELLA, *Nicola or Niccolo (REGGINELLI)*, A soprano singer of considerable repute, whose exact identity is in doubt. Burney records his appearance in London in 1746, when he says, "Reginelli, an old but great singer, whose voice, as well as his person, was in ruin, first appeared. . .This person was now turned of fifty; his voice was a soprano but cracked, and in total decay." Handel wrote the famous *Ombra cara* for him, according to Burney. And he engaged in a duel with Caffarelli over who was the most vain and arrogant; a draw, 1739.

REICHART, *Johann Friedrich (REICHARDT)*, 1752-1814. A composer and student of G. G. Richter, appointed Kapell-meister to Frederick II at Potsdam in 1775, and dismissed in 1794 for pro-revolutionary sympathies. He composed numerous operas and singspiels, as well as songs and miscellaneous instrumental works. K. P. E. Bach was also at Potsdam at this time. Reichardt was extremely active, and his literary output almost equals his musical output.

REUTTER, *Teresa di*. Nothing can be found about this singer.

RICCIERI, *Giovanni Antonio (RICIERI)*, 1679-1744. A soprano castrato, student of Freschi, Alghisi, and Bassani, who made his debut in 1700. From 1701 he was the soloist at San Petronio in Bologna, where Perti was *maestro di cappella*, and a student of Pistocchi. He turned to composition, and was quite critical of his fellow Accademia members. From 1722-26 he was in Poland as composer, then returned to Bologna to teach composition, where Padre Martini was a student. His character seems to have been contentious.

SALA, *Niccola*, 1713-1801. A composer, theorist and singing master who studied with Fago, Abos and Leo. His compositions include many operas, plus oratorios, masses, etc. A work on counterpoint was considered for many years his most important achievement.

SALIERI, *Antonio*, 1750-1825. A composer, tenor singer, who studied with his brother Francesco, as well as Simoni, Pescetti and Pacini. Gassmann was his patron for many years, and provided for his education in composition in Vienna from 1766. His first operas being successful, Salieri gave up singing and upon Gassmann's sudden death in 1774, succeeded him as court composer in Vienna. Gluck also patronised him to his advantage, and the story of great rivalry with Mozart seems to be enlarged out of all proportion. Beethoven, Schubert, and Liszt all studied with him.

SALIMBENE, *Felice (SALIMBENI)*, 1712-1751. A soprano castrato, student of Porpora, who made his debut in 1731. Great fame and wealth attached themselves to this castrato, who spent a good portion of his time in royal service: Charles VI (Vienna), 1733-39; Frederick II (Potsdam), 1743-50; then to Dresden in 1751. His voice was said to be of surpassing beauty and great range, with especial advantage in 'rendering adagios.' His person was extremely handsome.

SANDONI, *Pietro*, c. 1680-c. 1750. A harpsichordist, composer and singing master who resided in London about 1714, if he is the same Sandoni who gave Mrs. Anastasia Robinson vocal lessons (Burney). Certainly he was the husband of Cuzzoni, and rival of Handel, mentioned in much of the correspondence of the time.

SANTARELLI, *Giuseppe*, 1710-90. A soprano castrato, *maestro di cappella* of the Papal Chapel and acquaintance of Burney's during his travels in Italy. Santarelli was quite helpful to Burney in obtaining documentation from Papal Archives on musical questions. He was also the author of a work on church music history, only the first volume of which was published.

SARRO, *Domenico (SARRI)*, c. 1678- after 1739. A composer with a European reputation without ever leaving the service of the Chapel Royal in Naples. He wrote 36 operas, plus oratorios, masses, etc.

SCALZI, *Carlo*, c. 1695- ??. A good second-rank castrato, constantly employed. He appeared from 1734 among Handel's singers in London with success, but not overwhelmingly so. He was a second man in London, but Burney quotes Mancini's edition of 1774 in respect to Scalzi having risen to the top of the profession after his years in London. Little else is known of him.

SCARLATTI, *Alessandro*, 1660-1725. A composer and teacher of singing, he studied with Carissimi. In 1679, his first opera was produced in Rome. He is reputed to have written about 115 operas, 200 masses, numerous oratorios, and

additional music for this and that. He could count most of
the musicians of his day among his students, including Hasse
and Handel. He is a founder and cornerstone of the Neapolitan school of opera.

[Senesino], *BERNARDI, Francesco,* c. 1680-c. 1750. A
soprano castrato and student of Bernacchi. He called himself
Senesino after his birthplace, Siena. He came to London for
Handel's troupe in 1720, and was enormously successful. He
stayed until 1735. Senesino and Cuzzoni were antagonistic
to Handel, and it was largely because of their antagonism
that Porpora was invited to come to London. Quantz calls
him a contralto, and praises him greatly in all the matters
which made up a great singer.

[Siface], *GROSSI, Giovanni Francesco,* 1653-1697. A
soprano castrato, whose numerous amorous affairs made him
notorious and finally resulted in his murder. He appeared
in London in 1687, the first castrato to sing there, although
he did not appear in public performances. He was immensely
popular with the nobility, however. He was extremely handsome and vain, and was considered something of a lady's 'man.'
It seems firmly established that his cognomen comes from
his appearance in Cavalli's opera *Scipione Africano,* 1678,
in the part of Syphax. He was a student of Tomaso Redi.

STEFFANI, Giuseppe (STEFFAN, Joseph Anton), 1726-97.
A composer and teacher of singing. He studied with Wagenseil, and was the teacher of Marie Antoinette and Caroline
(later Queen of Naples). He wrote many songs, considered
among the best of his time.

TARTAGLINI, Rosa, died 9 September 1775. The wife of
Giuseppe Tibaldi, tenor.

TARTINI, Giuseppe, 1692-1770. A composer, violinist and
theorist. He studied with Padre Czernohorsky, 'il Padre
Boemo'. In 1728, he established a violin school in Padua,
from which issued many of the most famous virtuosi of the
time. He composed numerous concerti, etc., for the violin.

TENDUCCI, Giusto Ferdinando, c. 1736- died after 1800.
A soprano castrato who made his debut in 1753. In 1758, he
arrived in London as second man, but soon eclipsed Potenza,
and took over the first position. Tenducci's fame rests on
the fact that he was the center of a great scandel, for he
married Miss Dora Maunsell, and the resulting storm landed
him in jail. The marriage was annulled in 1775. Tenducci
then settled in London, where he remained until 1791, teaching
singing. In about 1785, he published *Instructions of Mr.
Tenducci to His Students,* the maxims of which reappear, without change, in Aprile's *Modern Italian Method,* 1791. Tenducci
had left London by this time. He also composed operas.
Occasionally he was known as Senesino, having been born in

Siena.

TESI, *Vittoria (Tesi-Tramontini)*, 1700-75. A contralto and student of Campeggi. Her voice was remarkable for its depth and power, and her best roles were male travesty roles. Handel deplored her questionable taste in singing bass arias up an octave. Her personal character was not above reproach, but her artistic qualities seem to have been quite high. Quantz heard her and admired the fire and force of her singing, although she lacked the fioratura which made Faustina so famous.

TEYBER, *Elisabeth* [Die Teuberin], 1748- died after 1788. A soprano, student of Tesi and Hasse, who sang in and around Vienna. She made a trip to Russia, which caused the complete loss of her voice. Upon return to warmer climates, it reappeared. Her sister, Therese, was the first Blonde in Mozart's *Die Entfuhrung Aus Dem Serail*, 1782.

TIBALDI, *Giuseppe Luigi*, 1719, died after 1772. A tenor singer and composer, considered one of the greatest singers of his day. He was elected to the Accademia Filarmonica in 1747. He then began to study singing, and became an international star. In 1759, he was Principal of the Accademia. He was the husband of the soprano Rosa Tartaglini. The last record of his appearances was in Bologna in 1772. He is apparently a member of the Bolognese family Tibaldi which produced no less than three leading tenors in one generation.

TOSCHI. Nothing could be located under Toschi. However, there was a large family by the name of *TOESCHI*, associated with the Mannheim Orchestra during the latter half of the eighteenth and early nineteenth centuries. All of them wrote chamber and instrumental music. They were: Carlo Giuseppe, 1722-88; Giovanni Battista, 1727-1800; and Carlo Teodoro, 1765-1835.

TOZZI, *Antonio*, 1736- died after 1812. A composer who studied with Padre Martini, and wrote a good deal of chamber and church music in addition to operas. In 1773, *Zenobia*, text by Metastasio, came out in Munich. In 1765, he was *maestro di cappella* to the Duke of Brunswick, and in Spain from 1788-92. He was Principal of the Accademia Filarmonica in 1769.

TRAJETTA, *Tommaso (TRAETTA)*, 1727-1779. A composer and student of Durante. His first opera was produced in 1751. In 1758, he entered the service of Prince of Parma as composer and singing master to the princesses. 1768-75 was spent in Russia at the court. Then in London, where his operas were greatly successful. He wrote 48 operas in all, with a sense of drama and melodic gift. He was immensely well-regarded by his contemporaries.

VALENTE, *Saverio*, fl. c. 1750. A Neapolitan composer,

trained at the Pieta. He was *maestro di cappella* at San
Francesco Severio, Naples. He left considerable church music
and a counterpoint method.

VASQUEZ, *Giambattista*. Nothing is known of this singer
beside the scant information Mancini gives. He was born in
Domaso, near Lake Como, and sang in the Court at Lisbon.

VINCI, *Leonardo*, 1690-1730. A composer who studied
with Greco. He was chiefly associated with the chapel at
Naples and remained there until his death. About 40 operas
in addition to other works contain his output.

VISCONTI, *Caterina* [la Viscontina]. Burney described
her as having a 'shrill flexible voice, and pleased more in
rapid songs than in those that required high colouring and
pathos.' She was born in Milan, student of G. F. Brivio.
Mancini's opinion is much higher than Burney's and he may
have known her earlier.

WAGENSEIL, *Georg Christoph*, 1715-1777. A composer and
theorist who studied with J. J. Fux. In 1739, he was appointed court composer in Vienna. Many Italian operas by him,
were produced in Vienna and other areas. In addition, other
compositions for voices and instruments, were forthcoming.
He was highly regarded in his profession.

ZONDADARI, *Cav. Sig. Marchese Fulvio Ghigi of Siena*.
Nothing can be found regarding this illustrious amateur, beyond what Mancini tells us. One can surmise that Ghigi is
either misspelled, or is an earlier form of Chigi, and that
there is a connection with the wealthy Sienese family of
that name.